TOEIC® TEST LISTENING & READING

With free audio, script, and answer key

Hosam Elmetaher

Copyright © 2017 Hosam Elmetaher

All rights reserved.

ISBN: 9781549701696

LICENSE NOTES

This textbook may not be re-sold or given away to other people. If you would like to share this textbook with another person, please purchase an additional copy for each recipient. If you are reading this textbook and did not purchase it, or it was not purchased for your use only, then please return to your favorite textbook retailer and purchase your own copy. Thank you for respecting the hard work of the author.

ACKNOWLEDGMENTS

I would like to express my sincere gratitude to those who have enriched my academic and professional skills.
THANK YOU

CONTENTS

1. Preface — Pg #1
2. Introduction — Pg #2
3. Test overview — Pg #3
4. TOEIC® listening — Pg #4
5. TOEIC® listening: Part 1 (photographs) — Pg #5
6. TOEIC® listening: Part 2 (question-response) — Pg #20
7. TOEIC® listening: Part 3 (conversations) — Pg #27
8. TOEIC® listening: Part 4 (talks) — Pg #59
9. TOEIC® reading — Pg #88
10. TOEIC® reading: Part 5 (incomplete sentences) — Pg #89
11. TOEIC® reading: Part 6 (text completion) — Pg #109
12. TOEIC® reading: Part 7 (comprehension) — Pg #125
13. Appendix: Frequently asked questions — Pg #159
14. Appendix: Test day tips — Pg #160
15. Appendix: Contact us — Pg #161

PREFACE

Book description

This is a full TOEIC® course that has already helped hundreds of students from all over the world to achieve high scores in the TOEIC® test. This textbook has been carefully designed, developed, and tested to meet all your TOEIC® needs. It contains an explanation of each part of the test, TOEIC® strategies, vocabulary words, lots of practice questions, and an answer key with free audio and script.

What is special about this book?

- *Extensive*: Covers all the necessary TOEIC® skills.
- *Authentic*: Similar questions to the real TOEIC® test.
- *Easy to use*: Contains English understandable for lower level English students.
- *Comprehensive*: Includes explanations, language and TOEIC® skills, practice questions, and an answer key with free audio and script.
- *Good for self-study*: No teacher needed! The book is easy to follow.

INTRODUCTION

What is TOEIC® TEST?

TOEIC stands for *"Test of English for International Communication."* It is a paper and pencil test containing 100-multiple choice listening questions divided into four sections, and another 100-multiple choice reading questions divided into three sections. Basically, the test consists of a total of 200-multiple choice questions that should be answered in two hours. The TOEIC® test differs from the TOEFL® and IELTS® tests as follows:

- It tests business English.
- It contains no writing or speaking components.*
- It is used mainly for job hunting.
- It has a maximum score of 990:- 495 for listening and 495 for reading.

*Note: There is a new version of the TOEIC® test that tests speaking and writing, but the listening and reading test is the most common one.

Sample TOEIC® Score Certificate

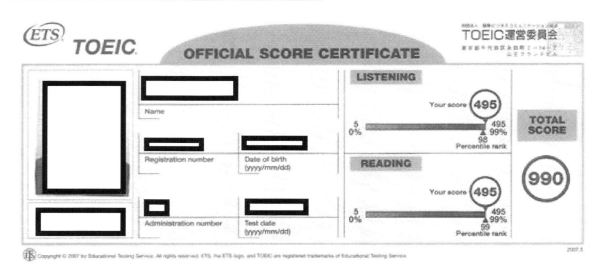

TEST OVERVIEW

TOEIC® test has 100 listening questions and 100 reading questions. We will go through each section in more detail.

TOEIC® Test			
	Listening	**Reading**	**Total**
Number of questions	100 questions	100 questions	200 questions
Time	45 minutes	75 minutes	120 minutes
Maximum score	495 points	495 points	990 points
Minimum score	5 points	5 points	10 points

TOEIC Listening

As of May 2016, the listening section has **100** questions to be completed in **45** minutes. All questions are multiple choice and are divided into four parts.
- Part 1: Photographs, **6** questions.
- Part 2: Question-Response, **25** questions.
- Part 3: Conversations (with and without a visual image), **39** questions.
- Part 4: Talks (with and without a visual image), **30** questions.

TOEIC Reading

As of May 2016, the reading section consists of **100** questions to be completed in **75** minutes. All the questions are multiple choice and are divided into three parts.
- Part 5: Incomplete sentences, **30** questions.
- Part 6: Text Completion, **16** questions.
- Part 7: Reading Comprehension, **54** questions.

Notes

....
....
....
....
....
....
....
....
....
....
....
....

TOEIC LISTENING

How to use this section of the book?

1. Listen to the free audio at https://goo.gl/k4mdMJ
2. Read the answer options, if any.
3. Choose the best answer.
5. Check your answer(s).
6. Look at the answer's explanation, and study TOEIC ® tips.
7. Practice!

PART 1: PHOTOGRAPHS

(6 QUESTIONS)

In this section you will see a photo and listen to four statements. You need to choose either A, B, C, or D for the sentence that best describes the photo and record it in your answer sheet. You will not see written sentences and the audio will be played only once.

Example:
In the test book, you may see the following picture.

You will then hear four statements about the picture. Only one of them is correct. You may hear the following:

A. They are staring at a computer screen.
B. They are discussing a business report.
C. They are playing a computer game.
D. They are typing an email.

Answer:
The correct answer is A. "They are staring (looking) at a computer screen." Therefore, you should select and mark "A" in your answer sheet.

Strategies:

Before the audio starts, quickly look at the photo and try to think of the three main WH questions – who, where, and what. For example, imagine a photo of a woman shopping at a supermarket for practice:

Who? A young woman and a sales person.
Where? A supermarket.
What: A woman shopping.

Hint

Don't choose an answer that has a similar sound or word to what you see in the picture. For example, for the previous picture of a woman shopping at the market, you may see the following possible answers:

A. A woman is shoplifting
B. Women are shopping
C. There are few products in the shop
D. A lady is buying some stuff

Let's assume that you couldn't understand any of the previous four possible answers, but; 'A' includes the word, "shoplifting," which is close to the word "shopping." However, this is not the right answer. 'B' has the words, "women," and, "shopping," both of which are similar to what you see in the picture. However, 'B' is not the correct answer. 'C' states that the shop has few products. Well, logically it is a shop which is usually full of products, so no, this is not the correct answer. 'D' uses words like, "lady," and, "buying," which might well describe the picture, so this is the correct answer. Again, don't forget, the test will give different words you might expect to hear, but they are, usually, not the correct answers.

Notes

20 Practice Questions: Listen to the audio, and circle your answer.

Listen to the audio, and circle your answer.

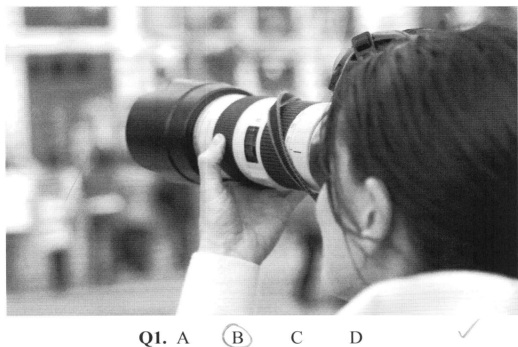

Q1. A (B) C D ✓

Q2. A B C (D) ✓

Listen to the audio, and circle your answer.

Q3. A (B) C D

Q4. (A) B C D

Listen to the audio, and circle your answer.

Q5. A B C (D)

Q6. A B (C) D

Listen to the audio, and circle your answer.

Q7. A   B   Ⓒ   D

Q8. Ⓐ   B   C   D

Listen to the audio, and circle your answer.

Q9. A   B   Ⓒ   D   ✓

Q10. Ⓐ   B   C   D   ✓

TOEIC® Test: Listening & Reading

Listen to the audio, and circle your answer.

Q11. A (B) C D ✓

Q12. (A) B C D ✓

Listen to the audio, and circle your answer.

Q13. A B (C) D ✓

Q14. A (B) C D f

Listen to the audio, and circle your answer.

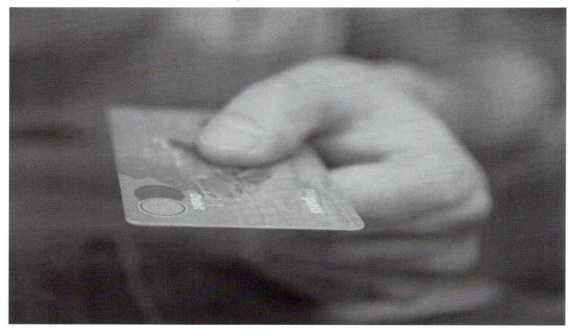

Q15. (A)　B　C　D　✓

Q16. (A)　B　C　D

Listen to the audio, and circle your answer.

Q17. (A)　　B　　C　　D　　✓

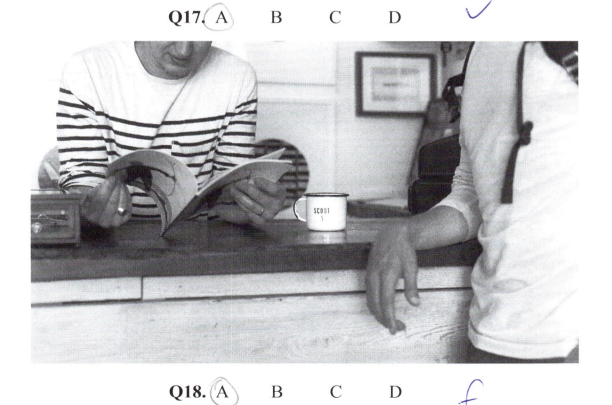

Q18. (A)　　B　　C　　D

Listen to the audio, and circle your answer.

Q19. A   B   (C)   D   ✓

Q20. (A)   B   C   D   f

SCRIPT & ANSWER KEY: Q1 – Q20

Q1.
- A. The woman is looking at the picture.
- B. <u>The woman is taking a picture.</u>
- C. The woman is checking the view.
- D. The woman is buying a new camera.

Q2.
- A. They are watching the field.
- B. They have a cow race.
- C. They are training a wild cow.
- D. <u>They are plowing the field.</u>

Q3.
- A. They are dating.
- B. They are quarreling.
- C. They are travelling.
- D. <u>They are having a discussion.</u>

Q4.
- A. <u>Vegetables can be purchased here.</u>
- B. This is a floating market.
- C. You have to pay in cash only.
- D. This is a very crowded market.

Q5.
- A. The man is repairing his computer.
- B. The man is filling out an application.
- C. The man is relaxing in the sunshine.
- D. <u>The man is working on his personal PC.</u>

Q6.
- A. They are lying on the desks.
- B. They are purchasing computers.
- C. <u>They are office staff.</u>
- D. They are police officers.

Q7.
- A. They are faking a report.
- B. They are writing a report.
- C. <u>They are examining a report.</u>
- D. They are discarding a report.

Q8.
- A. <u>The man is staring at his laptop.</u>
- B. The man is making himself comfortable.
- C. The man is checking his email.
- D. The man is switching off his computer.

Q9.
- A. He is a pianist.
- B. He is playing with a guitar.
- C. <u>He is playing a guitar.</u>
- D. He is selling his guitar.

Q10.
- A. <u>She is using a touch screen device.</u>
- B. She bought a new tablet.
- C. She is submitting her final report.
- D. She has desktop computer.

Q11.
- A. A chef is slicing meat.
- B. <u>A chef is preparing a meal.</u>
- C. A chef is making a table.
- D. A chef is chopping onions.

Q12.
- A. <u>The airplane is taking off.</u>
- B. The airplane is landing.
- C. The airplane is crashing.
- D. The airplane is sinking.

Q13.
- A. This is a line of motorbikes.
- B. Bicycles are for sale.
- C. <u>This is a queue of bikes.</u>
- D. People forgot their bikes.

Q14.
- A. This is a casual meeting.
- B. This is an informal meeting.
- C. <u>This is a formal meeting.</u>
- D. This is a long-distance meeting.

Q15.
   A. <u>The man is purchasing something.</u>
   B. The man is approaching.
   C. The man is using cash.
   D. The man is shopping online.

Q16.
   A. <u>The city is full of skyscrapers.</u>
   B. There are many crowded townhouses.
   C. This is the countryside.
   D. This is a beach city.

Q17.
   A. <u>Two people are exchanging notes.</u>
   B. Two people are gossiping.
   C. Two people are reporting.
   D. Two people are using their smartphones.

Q18.
   A. A man is selling magazines.
   B. <u>He is scanning a magazine.</u>
   C. He is a magazine editor.
   D. He is looking for a food recipe.

Q19.
   A. She hangs up the phone.
   B. She is restarting her phone.
   C. <u>She is on the phone.</u>
   D. She is using an earpiece.

Q20.
   A. This is a family meeting.
   B. <u>This is an informal meeting.</u>
   C. She is going to fire the man.
   D. The man is a new employee.

16 / 20

PART 2: QUESTION-RESPONSE

(25 QUESTIONS)

In this part of the test, you will hear a question or statement and three possible answers. You need to mark either A, B, or C to provide the best answer to the statement or question. Again, you won't see either the question, statement, or the three possible answers. So you need to listen carefully to all of them and mark the correct answer in your answer sheet.

Example:

In the audio you may hear: Where is the meeting room?
Next, you may hear three possible answers as follows:
A. To meet new friends.
B. To rest or to relax.
C. It's on the first floor on the left.

Answer:

Clearly, the correct answer is C. "It's on the first floor on the left."

Strategies

If you hear a statement (sentence), try to avoid the answer that has words or sounds that are similar to the statement. So, in other words, don't choose any answer that has some similar sounds or words to the questions that you heard.
As an example:
Q. How are you today?
   A. It is today
   B. How it is
   C. It is fine weather
   D. I can't complain

The correct answer is D. Even though, you might feel it is uncommon answer, as the most common way to answer, 'how are you today?' is 'I am fine, thank you.' Answer 'A' has the word 'today'; answer 'B' has the word 'how'; and answer 'C' has the word 'fine.' So again, the test will not give you very easy answers to choose from.

Hint

If the sentence you hear is a question, then the question word makes it easier for you. For example, if the question starts with, "when," then the answer must have a time or date. If it started with, "can," then the answer should have in it, "can," or, "can't," and so on!

38 Practice Questions: Listen to the audio, and circle your answer.

Q21.	A	(B)	C ✓	Q40.	A	B	(C) ✓
Q22.	A	B	(C) ✓	Q41.	A	B	(C) ✓
Q23.	A	(B)	C ✓	Q42.	(A)	B	C ✓
Q24.	A	B	(C) ✓	Q43.	(A)	B	C ✓
Q25.	(A)	B	C ✓	Q44.	A	(B)	C ✓
Q26.	A	(B)	C ✓	Q45.	(A)	B	C ✓
Q27.	A	B	(C) ✓	Q46.	A	(B)	C ✓
Q28.	(A)	B	C f	Q47.	A	B	(C) ✓
Q29.	A	(B)	C ✓	Q48.	A	B	(C) f
Q30.	A	B	(C) ✓	Q49.	A	(B)	C ✓
Q31.	(A)	B	C ✓	Q50.	A	B	(C) f
Q32.	A	(B) f	C f	Q51.	(A)	B	C ✓
Q33.	(A) f	B	C f	Q52.	A	(B)	C ✓
Q34.	A	(B)	C ✓	Q53.	A	B	(C) ✓
Q35.	(A)	B	C ✓	Q54.	A	B	(C) ✓
Q36.	A	B	(C) ✓	Q55.	(A)	B	C ✓
Q37.	A	(B)	C ✓	Q56.	(A)	B	C ✓
Q38.	A	(B)	C f	Q57.	A	(B)	C ✓
Q39.	(A)	B	C ✓	Q58.	(A)	B	C ✓

32/38

SCRIPT & ANSWER KEY: Q21- Q25

Q21. Thanks for the dinner invitation on Friday.
  A. How about Thursday?
  B. <u>Don't mention it.</u>
  C. I would say.

Q22. Would you like a cup of coffee?
  A. No, cocoa please.
  B. Coffee please.
  C. <u>Please!</u>

Q23. Do you need a break?
  A. He broke his leg.
  B. <u>A few minutes would do!</u>
  C. Yes, they do.

Q24. Would you like to join us for dinner?
  A. Dinner is at 7pm.
  B. He likes beef.
  C. <u>With pleasure!</u>

Q25. I don't like this car very much.
  A. <u>Neither do I!</u>
  B. Ok, it will do.
  C. Yes, it is good car.

Q26. Do you think I should still submit my paper? The deadline was yesterday, you know!
  A. You do?
  B. <u>Better late than never!</u>
  C. The deadline is approaching.

Q27. Hurry up! We will miss the train.
  A. It will be missed.
  B. The train was late.
  C. <u>Easy does it!</u>

Q28. I am really tired of my new job.
 A. <u>Hang in there!</u>
 B. So am I.
 C. You need a new tire.

Q29. It is going to be sunny tomorrow.
 A. Time for a nap.
 B. <u>Why don't we go hiking then!</u>
 C. It is unpredictable.

Q30. Do you think I need to take leave?
 A. I would leave.
 B. Yes, you live.
 C. <u>Have you consulted your boss?</u>

Q31. Too many headaches, I can't work anymore!
 A. <u>Why don't you take a break!</u>
 B. He isn't here anymore.
 C. Do you need headphones?

Q32. Did you see my bracelet? I can't find it.
 A. Thank you!
 B. Yes, she was here.
 C. <u>Did you ask around?</u>

Q33. Did you submit the report?
 A. Yes, I do.
 B. No, he isn't here.
 C. <u>In few minutes.</u>

Q34. How much is the bill?
 A. Not at all.
 B. <u>Your purchases added up to $536.26.</u>
 C. I need a bill too.

Q35. Can you get in the car?
 A. <u>Yes, if you just back up a little bit.</u>
 B. Yes, I can buy a new car.
 C. Yes, I parked my car.

Q36. Where is Jessica?
   A. In the washing machine.
   B. I am not Jessica
   C. <u>Her car broke down in the snowstorm.</u>

Q37. Are you OK? You look really pale!
   A. He is OK.
   B. <u>It is the flu.</u>
   C. I am thinking of a plan.

Q38. Would you like to meet my new colleagues, Tom and Chris?
   A. <u>Absolutely!</u>
   B. I appreciate it.
   C. Yes, I have new colleagues.

Q39. This is really delicious. Did you make it yourself?
   A. <u>My grandma did.</u>
   B. It is delicious.
   C. I agree with you.

Q40. Aren't you excited to meet our new manager?
   A. Let's meet tomorrow then.
   B. I love excitement.
   C. <u>Not really!</u>

Q41. Do you know who is attending the meeting?
   A. I don't have a meeting today.
   B. Yes, I am going for a meeting.
   C. <u>Nope!</u>

Q42. I would never work in this coffee shop again.
   A. <u>Never say never!</u>
   B. Coffee is a good idea.
   C. Yes, we will never shop again.

Q43. The show was hilarious, wasn't it?
   A. <u>You can say that again.</u>
   B. Did you see Hillary?
   C. Let's stop the show

Q44. I am not participating in tomorrow's workshop.
  A. Yes, I am.
  B. <u>Neither am I.</u>
  C. The workshop is at 9am.

Q45. Shall I lock the office before I go for lunch?
  A. <u>Don't worry about it.</u>
  B. I have a new locker.
  C. I have keys.

Q46. I had so much fun at the swimming pool yesterday.
  A. The swimming pool is next to our office.
  B. <u>Oh, so you can swim!</u>
  C. She can swim as well.

Q47. Where will our next meeting take place?
  A. Our last meeting was in the meeting room.
  B. Are you sure about it?
  C. <u>It is not confirmed yet</u>

Q48. The new employees look so energetic, motived, and ready for their working life.
  A. <u>To me, they actually look anxious.</u>
  B. We have many employees.
  C. Yes, they are retired.

Q49. Do you know the bus schedule?
  A. Yes, I know him.
  B. <u>The next one is at 2:50</u>.
  C. No, I don't have the flight schedule.

Q50. I only have $10; do you have any cash?
  A. We can pay by cash.
  B. <u>Well, that makes $25.</u>
  C. How much do you have?

Q51. If I was in your shoes, I wouldn't rent a shared room.
  A. <u>Why not?</u>
  B. I like my shoes.
  C. Let's share the room.

Q52. If this child could see, his life would be much easier.
  A. He is blind.
  B. <u>Indeed.</u>
  C. It is very easy.

Q53. I don't like unclean offices.
  A. He doesn't.
  B. Yes, it is.
  C. <u>Me neither!</u>

Q54. Do you feel comfortable in this new restaurant?
  A. Yes, he does.
  B. Yes, she does.
  C. <u>Yes, I do.</u>

Q55. Not everyone would handle living in a foreign country with ease.
  A. <u>I couldn't agree with you more!</u>
  B. I agree with you more.
  C. Let's live abroad.

Q56. I spent more than five hours setting up this new computer.
  A. <u>It's not rocket science!</u>
  B. Five more hours please.
  C. I agree with you.

Q57. Oh my! I failed again!
  A. I knew you could make it.
  B. <u>Just pull yourself together.</u>
  C. Congratulations.

Q58. Do you smoke?
  A. <u>I rarely do.</u>
  B. Yes, she does.
  C. I will be happy to help you.

PART 3: CONVERSATIONS

(39 QUESTIONS)

In this part of the test you will hear a conversation between two people. You will then be asked to answer three questions based on what you understand. You will see the question and the four possible answers, but you won't see the audio script. The audio will be played only once. You need to mark either A, B, C or D as the best answer to each question.

Example:
You could hear the following conversation.
Man: My computer broke again this afternoon. Why does this happen so often?
Woman: Don't worry. You can call the Help Desk and they will take care of it. You know, my PC is also not performing well, so I might need to call them too.
Man: But I need to submit this report in the next few hours. Can I use your computer for couple of minutes?
Woman: Go ahead!

Q1. What is the man's problem?
(A) He doesn't like his computer.
(B) His computer isn't working.
(C) His printer doesn't work.
(D) He is busy in the afternoon.
Answer: The correct answer is B. "His computer isn't working." He said that his computer is "broke" which means 'not working.'

Q2. What does the man have to submit?
(A) A report
(B) A presentation
(C) A meeting agenda
(D) An email
Answer: The correct answer is A. "A report."

Q3. What will the man most likely do next?
(A) Call his boss.
(B) Use the woman's PC.
(C) Wait until his PC has been fixed.
(D) Take a rest.

Answer: The correct answer is B. "Use the woman's PC." The man asked the woman if it is ok to use her PC for few minutes, and she agreed by saying "Go ahead!"

Strategies:
Try to quickly scan the questions and the four possible answers before the audio starts. This way, you will have an idea as to the kind of information that might be required. While listening to the audio, try to have another quick look over the questions and the four possible answers. The questions should be in the same order as the audio. Try not to spend too much time on any one question because the audio can't be repeated or paused.

Hint
This type of question usually asks about jobs, things people do, times, numbers (years, months, money, days), places, and reasons. Focus on those things as you are listening.

Notes

26 / 45

36 Practice Questions: Listen to the audio, and circle your answer.

Conversation 1

Q59. What's the main topic of the conversation?
   A. Writing a report.
   C. Report inquiry.
   B. Formal meeting.
   D. Work regulations.

Q60. Who is Mary?
   A. Employer.
   B. Employee.
   C. Supervisor.
   D. Student.

Q61. What will Mary probably do next?
   A. Re-submit the report.
   B. Nothing.
   C. Meet Mr. Williams again.
   D. Work on her weaknesses.

Script & Answer: Conversation 1

Woman: Mr. Williams, can I have a minute of your time please?
Man: Sure Mary, what's on your mind?
Woman: **(Q59)** I would like to talk with you about my last job evaluation report. I was wondering why I got such a low score.
Man: Well, let me see the report. Did you bring it with you?
Woman: Yes, here it is.
Man: Hmmm, this is quite confidential to share with you, but **(Q60)** I can see that this is your first year of employment in our company, you know. New employees might miss some important regulations, and that's probably what affected your total performance score.
Woman: How do you think I could improve on this point?
Man: **(Q61)** There are several ways to handle this. I would recommend, however, you talk with your senior colleagues, and/or the HR office.
Woman: Thank you Mr. Williams. I'll try my best.

Q59. What's the main topic of the conversation?
　　　A. Writing a report.
　　　B. Formal meeting.
　　　C. Report inquiry.
　　　D. Work regulations.

Q60. Who is Mary?
　　　A. Employer.
　　　B. Employee.
　　　C. Supervisor.
　　　D. Student.

Q61. What will Mary probably do next?
　　　A. Re-submit the report.
　　　B. Nothing.
　　　C. Meet Mr. Williams again.
　　　D. Work on her weaknesses.

Conversation 2

Q62. What's the main topic of the conversation?
  ✗ A. Working abroad.
  B. School tuition. ✓
  C. European English system.
  D. Summer vacation.

Q63. Who is Matt?
  A. Supervisor.
  B. Student.
  ✗ C. International employee.
  D. Co-worker.

Q64. What will Diana probably do next? ✓
  A. Ask for higher salary.
  ✗ B. Find a new job.
  C. Find a new local company.
  D. Find an inspiration.

Script & Answer: Conversation 2

Woman: Hey Matt, do you have a minute?
Man: Hi Diana, what's up?
Woman: Did you hear about a salary decrease? **(Q63)** <u>Our salary is already low. I am not sure if I can survive with that anymore, how about you?</u>
Man: This is the third time in a row. The company is receiving good profits, but are always complaining that income is not stable. **(Q62)** <u>I am considering working abroad.</u>
Woman: Really? Tell me more.
Man: In Europe, for example, most jobs are well-paid, and guess what, this also applies to international workers, with a good benefits package.
Woman: But why does Europe offer such quality jobs for foreign workers?
Man: The European government is highly supportive of skilled workers, but on the other hand, living in Europe is really expensive, and there are also limited English-based services.
Woman: **(Q64)** <u>I wouldn't mind learning a new language, and, of course, I would love to live in Europe. Thank you for the inspiration!</u>

Q62. What's the main topic of the conversation?
    A. <u>Working abroad.</u>
    B. School tuition.
    C. European English system.
    D. Summer vacation.

Q63. Who is Matt?
    A. Supervisor.
    B. Student.
    C. International employee.
    D. <u>Co-worker.</u>

Q64. What will Diana probably do next?
    A. Ask for higher salary.
    B. <u>Find a new job.</u>
    C. Find a new local company.
    D. Find an inspiration.

Conversation 3

Q65. What are the speakers working on?
  A. A report.
  B. An orientation.
  C. A final project.
  D. A surprise party.

Q66. Why do the speakers try to change the meeting place?
  A. They want a new place to meet.
  B. The usual meeting room is unavailable.
  C. They will meet newcomers.
  D. They want to work more hours.

Q67. How will the other group members know about the new plan?
  A. The man will contact them.
  B. The woman will contact them.
  C. No one will contact them.
  D. They already know.

Script & Answer: Conversation 3

Man: Hey, did you hear that our next meeting has been postponed?
Woman: Really? What for?
Man: **(Q66)** Our usual conference room has been booked for newcomer orientation, and we don't have a venue to meet in now.
Woman: **(Q65)** But what about our final report? It's next week! We really need to get together to finalize it as soon as possible.
Man: You're probably right, but I'm out of ideas for places where we could meet. Do you know of anywhere that would be suitable?
Woman: We could meet in the cafeteria. It is not usually crowded after the lunch break.
Man: **(Q67)** That's great. Let me contact the other members and make sure it's okay with them.
Woman: Okay, just let me know once it's settled.
Man: OK, I will!

Q65. What are the speakers working on?
  A. A report.
  B. An orientation.
  C. A final project.
  D. A surprise party.

Q66. Why do the speakers try to change the meeting place?
  A. They want a new place to meet.
  B. The usual meeting room is unavailable.
  C. They will meet newcomers.
  D. They want to work more hours.

Q67. How will the other group members know about the new plan?
  A. The man will contact them.
  B. The woman will contact them.
  C. No one will contact them.
  D. They already know.

Conversation 4

Q68. Why does Paul want to meet with Mr. Smith?
    A. To talk about his report.
    B. To submit some documents. ✓
    C. To find out about next the next project.
    ✗D. To ask for advice.

Q69. What is Paul's main problem?
    A. Low work performance. ✓
    B. Salary issues.
    C. Competitive work environment.
    ✗D. The weather.

Q70. What will Paul probably do next?
    A. Talk with the HR office. ✓
    ✗B. Change his work schedule.
    C. Transfer to a new branch.
    D. Schedule a meeting with his director.

Script & Answer: Conversation 4

Man: Good morning Mrs. Smith. Can I schedule an appointment with you as soon as possible?
Woman: You look worried, Paul! What is going on? We can talk now if you want.
Man: **(Q68)** Thank you. I think I will transfer to a different branch, and I was wondering if you have any recommendations.
Woman: Oh ok, well, there are few branches with openings for your area of specialization, but why do you want to transfer? Any problems?
Man: Not at all, in fact I like all my job here and I received quite good work performance reports.
Woman: Great! So, what seems to be the problem? Oh, and do you know that all your years of experience might not be transferable. It really depends on the new branch. You might need to talk with their HR office to find out.
Man: Oh no, I don't want to lose any of my experience. **(Q69)** Well, it is about the weather. It is really burning hot here during the summer session!
Woman: Did you know that if you take overtime during the winter season, you will be eligible for a summer break.
Man: **(Q70)** Really? I might just check that out!

Q68. Why does Paul want to meet with Mr. Smith?
    A. To talk about his report.
    B. To submit some documents.
    C. To find out about next the next project.
    D. To ask for advice.

Q69. What is Paul's main problem?
    A. Low work performance.
    B. Salary issues.
    C. Competitive work environment.
    D. The weather.

Q70. What will Paul probably do next?
    A. Talk with the HR office.
    B. Change his work schedule.
    C. Transfer to a new branch.
    D. Schedule a meeting with his director.

Conversation 5

Q71. Which department should Sally contact?
    A. HR department.
    B. Marketing department.
    C. Customer Service department.
    D. Admin department.

Q72. What is the ad missing?
    A. Bigger font.
    B. Relevant graphic.
    C. Both A and B.
    D. None of the above.

Q73. Who is the man?
    A. The bellboy.
    B. A postal service representative.
    C. The manager.
    D. Marketing department staff.

Script & Answer: Conversation 5

Man: **(Q71)** Sally, would you mind asking the marketing department to create a better design for the newspaper ad?
Woman: Does it look that bad?
Man: **(Q72)** The font is too small, and the graphic is totally irrelevant!
Woman: **(Q73)** Sure, sir. I will get in touch with them right away.
Man: Thank you very much.

Q71. Which department should Sally contact?
  A. HR department.
  B. Marketing department.
  C. Customer Service department.
  D. Admin department.

Q72. What is the ad missing?
  A. Bigger font.
  B. Relevant graphic.
  C. Both A and B.
  D. None of the above.

Q73. Who is the man?
  A. The bellboy.
  B. A postal service representative.
  C. The manager.
  D. Marketing department staff.

Conversation 6

Q74. Where is the man?
- A. Convenience store.
- B. Mechanic shop.
- C. Clothing shop.
- D. Money exchange office.

Q75. What is the problem with the shirt?
- A. Large collar.
- B. Bigger size.
- C. Short sleeves.
- D. Cheap quality.

Q76. What will the man probably do?
- A. Receive 10% discount.
- B. Exchange the shirt.
- C. Buy a new shirt.
- D. Return the shirt.

Script & Answer: Conversation 6

Man: **(Q74)** I would like to return that shirt I bought yesterday. **(Q75)** The sleeves are too short.
Woman: Sure, but would you like to exchange it instead, with a 10% discount on the original price.
Man: **(Q76)** No, thanks. I bought a new one already, but I appreciate the offer.
Woman: No problem! Can I see the receipt please?
Man: Here you are.

Q74. Where is the man?
- A. Convenience store.
- B. Mechanic shop.
- C. Clothing shop.
- D. Money exchange office.

Q75. What is the problem with the shirt?
- A. Large collar.
- B. Bigger size.
- C. Short sleeves.
- D. Cheap quality.

Q76. What will the man probably do?
- A. Receive 10% discount.
- B. Exchange the shirt.
- C. Buy a new shirt.
- D. Return the shirt.

Conversation 7

Q77. What is the man name?
    A. Adam.
    B. Monica.
    C. Washington.
    D. Not mentioned.

Q78. How many times did the man and woman meet?
    A. One time.
    B. Two times.
    C. Three times.
    D. Four times.

Q79. What does the woman mean by saying, "same here"?
    A. She is living nearby.
    B. She doesn't remember the man.
    C. She is happy to see the man.
    D. She has to go.

Script & Answer: Conversation 7

Man: Sorry to interrupt, but, somehow, I recognize your face. Have we met before?
Woman: Hmmm, sorry, but I don't think so.
Man: Is your name Monica? **(Q78)** <u>I guess we met at Adam's wedding anniversary, in the Washington hotel.</u>
Woman: Oh yeah, I remember you now! How are you?
Man: I can't complain. It is really good to see you again.
Woman: **(Q79)** <u>Same here!</u>

Q77. What is the man name?
    A. Adam.
    B. Monica.
    C. Washington.
    D. <u>Not mentioned.</u>

Q78. How many times did the man and woman meet?
    A. <u>One time.</u>
    B. Two times.
    C. Three times.
    D. Four times.

Q79. What does the woman mean by saying, "same here"?
    A. She is living nearby.
    B. She doesn't remember the man.
    C. <u>She is happy to see the man.</u>
    D. She has to go.

Conversation 8

Q80. How far is the restaurant?
    A. About ten miles away.
    B. Within walking distance.
    C. In a nearby city.
    D. In Mexico.

Q81. What is chicken tostada?
    A. Vegetarian dish.
    B. Chicken meat with vegetables.
    C. Mix of chicken, beef, and pork meat.
    D. Mexican dessert.

Q82. What would the man probably do?
    A. Try a Minnesota restaurant.
    B. Find the restaurant address.
    C. Recommend a different restaurant
    D. Try the new restaurant

Script & Answer: Conversation 8

Man: I am starving!
Woman: Me too, how about trying something new. **(Q80)** <u>I heard about a new Mexican restaurant on the next block</u>.
Man: Sounds good! What do you recommend?
Woman: How about a chicken tostada?
Man: A chicken tostada?
Woman: (Q81) <u>It is an authentic Mexican dish that layers creamy refried beans, moist chicken, luscious avocado, and crisp shredded lettuce on top of a warm, crispy corn tortilla.</u>
Man: (Q82) <u>I can't wait to taste it.</u>

Q80. How far is the restaurant?
    A. About ten miles away.
    B. <u>Within walking distance.</u>
    C. In a nearby city.
    D. In Mexico.

Q81. What is chicken tostada?
    A. Vegetarian dish.
    B. <u>Chicken meat with vegetables.</u>
    C. Mix of chicken, beef, and pork meat.
    D. Mexican dessert.

Q82. What would the man probably do?
    A. Try a Minnesota restaurant.
    B. Find the restaurant address.
    C. Recommend a different restaurant.
    D. <u>Try the new restaurant</u>

Conversation 9

Q83. Who is the woman?
    A. Dermatologist.
    B. Surgeon.
    C. Pharmacist. ✓
    ✗ D. Dentist.

Q84. What is cause of the man pain?
    A. His teeth.
    B. His nose.
    ✗ C. His blood pressure.
    D. His headache.

Q85. What did the man feel in the end?
    A. Confused.
    B. Worried.
    C. Relaxed.
    ✗ D. None of the above.

Script & Answer: Conversation 9

Man: The pain in my front teeth is killing me!
Woman: **(Q83)** Please open your mouth wide and let me check it.
Man: I also get a headache once in a while.
Woman: **(Q84)** I guess the pain is probably caused by a sinus infection.
Man: Really?
Woman: I will prescribe a one-week prescription for you. The antibiotic should ease your pain.
Man: (Q85) What a relief.

Q83. Who is the woman?
    A. Dermatologist.
    B. Surgeon.
    C. Pharmacist.
    D. Dentist.

Q84. What is cause of the man pain?
    A. His teeth.
    B. His nose.
    C. His blood pressure.
    D. His headache.

Q85. What did the man feel in the end?
    A. Confused.
    B. Worried.
    C. Relaxed.
    D. None of the above.

Conversation 10

Q86. What is the relationship between the man and the woman?
   A. Brother and sister.
   B. Husband and wife.
   C. Colleagues.
   D. Friends.

Q87. What does the woman think about Pacific Ocean?
   A. She likes it.
   B. She hates it.
   C. She doesn't know where it is located.
   D. She has been there before.

Q88. What does the woman feel about relocating?
   A. She loves it.
   B. She is tired of it.
   C. She is happy about it.
   D. It is her first time doing it.

Script & Answer: Conversation 10

Man: (Q86) <u>Honey,</u> I have good news and bad news.
Woman: I'm listening.
Man: We will have a relaxing vacation on the Pacific Ocean.
Woman: (Q87) <u>How exciting.</u> But wait, what about the bad news.
Man: We have to relocate there.
Woman: (Q88) <u>Come on! Relocating again!</u>

Q86. What is the relationship between the man and the woman?
    A. Brother and sister.
    B. <u>Husband and wife.</u>
    C. Colleagues.
    D. Friends.

Q87. What does the woman think about Pacific Ocean?
    A. <u>She likes it.</u>
    B. She hates it.
    C. She doesn't know where it is located.
    D. She has been there before.

Q88. What does the woman feel about relocating?
    A. She loves it.
    B. <u>She is tired of it.</u>
    C. She is happy about it.
    D. It is her first time doing it.

Conversation 11

Q89. Where is the man going?
    A. Vending machine.
    B. Victoria Market.
    C. Victoria Square.
    D. Victoria Street.

Q90. Based on the woman directions, the man is probably……..?
    A. Walking.
    B. Driving.
    C. Using a taxi.
    D. Using the bus.

Q91. Why did the man say "you are a star"?
    A. He was flattering the woman.
    B. He is an astronomer.
    C. He likes stars.
    D. The place he is heading to is far away, like a star.

Script & Answer: Conversation 11

Man: Excuse me, I think I lost my way. **(Q89)** <u>Do you know how to get to Victoria Square?</u>
Woman: **(Q90)** <u>Yeah, the easiest way is to go right, after two traffic lights turn left, and then head straight for about two miles.</u>
Man: Thank you, and do you know if there is a vending machine around, as well. I feel a little thirsty.
Woman: I have a spare bottle of water. Here you are.
Man: (Q91) <u>You are a star.</u>

Q89. Where is the man going?
    A. Vending machine.
    B. Victoria Market.
    C. <u>Victoria Square.</u>
    D. Victoria Street.

Q90. Based on the woman directions, the man is probably…….?
    A. Walking.
    B. <u>Driving.</u>
    C. Using a taxi.
    D. Using the bus.

Q91. Why did the man say "you are a star"?
    A. <u>He was flattering the woman.</u>
    B. He is an astronomer.
    C. He likes stars.
    D. The place he is heading to is far away, like a star.

Conversation 12

Q92. How does the man feel about his visit to the White House?
  A. Nervous.
  B. Bored.
  C. Excited.
  D. Tired.

Q93. How many windows are there in the White House?
  A. 132.
  B. 412.
  C. 147.
  D. 28.

Q94. How did the woman know about the White House?
  A. From a brochure.
  B. From her friend, Jif.
  C. From a newspaper.
  D. From an online website.

Script & Answer: Conversation 12

Man: **(Q92)** <u>Wow! Finally, we can visit the White House.</u>
Woman: Did you know that the White House has 132 rooms, 35 bathrooms, and six levels? There are also 412 doors, **(Q93)** <u>147 windows,</u> 28 fireplaces, eight staircases, and three elevators.
Man: That's huge! But how do you know all that?
Woman: **(Q94)** <u>From *WhiteHouse.gov!*</u>

Q92. How does the man feel about his visit to the White House?
    A. Nervous.
    B. Bored.
    C. <u>Excited.</u>
    D. Tired.

Q93. How many windows are there in the White House?
    A. 132.
    B. 412.
    C. <u>147.</u>
    D. 28.

Q94. How did the woman know about the White House?
    A. From a brochure.
    B. From her friend, Jif.
    C. From a newspaper.
    D. <u>From an online website.</u>

Conversation 13

Q95. Where does the woman want to go?
    A. India.
    B. Thailand.
    C. Mountains.
    D. None of the above.

Q96. Which of the following the man might be more interested more in?
    A. Swimming.
    B. Surfing.
    C. Relaxing on the beach.
    D. Hiking.

Q97. Where did the man and woman agree to go?
    A. Thailand.
    B. India.
    C. Both Thailand and India.
    D. Not mentioned.

Script & Answer: Conversation 13

Man: Summer is approaching, don't you think we should go somewhere that has more fresh air?

Woman: **(Q95)** How about Thailand? I heard a lot about Phuket, an extremely attractive city with lots of things to do. You know, swimming, surfing, relaxing on the beach.

Man: **(Q96)** I am more into the mountain thing. How about India? We could enjoy hiking, cycling, and magnificent views!

Q95. Where does the woman want to go?
       A. India.
       B. Thailand.
       C. Mountains.
       D. None of the above.

Q96. Which of the following the man might be more interested more in?
       A. Swimming.
       B. Surfing.
       C. Relaxing on the beach.
       D. Hiking.

Q97. Where did the man and woman agree to go?
       A. Thailand.
       B. India.
       C. Both Thailand and India.
       D. Not mentioned.

Conversation 14

Q98. What is the problem with the printer?
    A. It doesn't turn on.
    B. It is not installed on the computer.
    C. It doesn't print.
    D. None of the above.

Q99. How much is the printer?
    A. 100 USD.
    B. 150 USD.
    C. 200 USD.
    D. 250 USD.

Q100. What will the man do?
    A. Visit her apartment.
    B. Call the woman again later.
    C. Send someone to help.
    D. Transfer her call to a technician.

Script & Answer: Conversation 14

Man: Hello, customer service. How can I help you today?
Woman: **(Q99)** Hello, it is about the 200 USD printer I bought yesterday. **(Q98)** It simply won't print.
Man: Did you check the power; make sure the printer is on; check to see that the printer is installed on your computer?
Woman: I did all that.
Man: **(Q100)** All right, we will send a technician to your apartment right away.

Q98. What is the problem with the printer?
    A. It doesn't turn on.
    B. It is not installed on the computer.
    C. It doesn't print.
    D. None of the above.

Q99. How much is the printer?
    A. 100 USD.
    B. 150 USD.
    C. 200 USD.
    D. 250 USD.

Q100. What will the man do?
    A. Visit her apartment.
    B. Call the woman again later.
    C. Send someone to help.
    D. Transfer her call to a technician.

Conversation 15

Q101. Why did the man and the woman decide to go shopping?
    A. It is the weekly shopping time.
    B. The vegetables are fresh.
    C. The market is near.
    D. They like to have a look.

Q102. Who will go first?
    A. The man.
    B. The woman.
    C. The man and the woman will go together.
    D. They won't go.

Q103. What does the woman mean by "please do"?
    A. The man should hurry.
    B. The man can have a snack.
    C. The man can go first.
    D. The man should wait for her.

Script & Answer: Conversation 15

Man: **(Q101)** It is harvest time, why don't we have a look in the vegetable market?
Woman: **(Q102)** Is it? Sure, let me get ready. You go ahead and I will be just behind you.
Man: Alright, do you mind if I have a snack till you arrive.
Woman: **(Q103)** Please do!

Q101. Why did the man and the woman decide to go shopping?
      A. It is the weekly shopping time.
      B. The vegetables are fresh.
      C. The market is near.
      D. They like to have a look.

Q102. Who will go first?
      A. The man.
      B. The woman.
      C. The man and the woman will go together.
      D. They won't go.

Q103. What does the woman mean by "please do"?
      A. The man should hurry.
      B. The man can have a snack.
      C. The man can go first.
      D. The man should wait for her.

PART 4: TALKS

(30 QUESTIONS)

In this part of the test you will listen to a short talk. You will then be asked to answer three questions based on what you have understood. You will see the question and the four possible answers but you won't see the audio script. The audio will only be played once. You need to mark either A, B, C, or D to provide the best answer for each question.

Example: In the audio you may hear:
We are glad to announce some new work benefits for our employees. All employees are now eligible for retirement benefits regardless of how long they have been working with us. Previously, only those who had spent 10 years or more were eligible to receive our retirement package. But now however, all of you will receive at least some of those benefits based on how long you have been working with us. So, rest assured that you won't be missing out.

Q1. Who is this announcement for?
(A) Students
(B) Company employees
(C) The public
(D) Tourists
Answer: The correct answer is B. "Company employees." In the first sentence, the speaker said that this is an announcement for "our employees"

Q2. What does the new change affect?
(A) Salary
(B) The retirement policy
(C) Insurance regulations
(D) The hiring process
Answer: The correct answer is B - "The retirement policy." The speaker said that "All employees are now eligible for the retirement benefits."

Q3. How long must you work to be eligible for the new policy?
(A) 10 years
(B) 5 years
(C) 1 year
(D) No specific period

Answer: The correct answer is D - "No specific period." The speaker mentioned that "All employees are now eligible for retirement benefits regardless of how long they have been working with us." This means there is no specified employment period to receive at least some retirement benefits.

Strategies:
As with the conversation questions, try to quickly read the questions and the four possible answers before you listen to the audio. This way, you will have an idea of the kind of information that will be required. While listening to the audio, try to have another quick look over the questions and the four possible answers. The questions should be in the same order as the audio. Very common questions types for this section include: Who is talking? What is he/she talking about? What is going to happen next? How long? How much? When will something happen?

Hint
These are quite straight forward types of questions. In other words, choose what you hear.

Notes

Practice

Talk 1

Q104. What is the topic mainly about?
- A. New York attractions.
- B. New York history.
- C. New York population.
- D. New York importance.

Q105. According to the speaker, what is the population of New York City?
- A. 8,550,405.
- B. 8,550,504.
- C. 8,450,505.
- D. 8,554,404.

Q106. According to the talk, New York City exerts a significant impact upon …..?
- A. Commerce, finance, and media.
- B. Art, fashion, and research.
- C. Technology, education, and entertainment.
- D. All the above.

Script & Answer: Talk 1

Woman: **(Q104)** The City of New York, often called New York City or simply New York, is the most populous city in the United States. **(Q105)** With an estimated 2015 population of 8,550,405 distributed over a land area of just 305 square miles (790 km2), New York City is also the most densely populated major city in the United States. Located at the southern tip of the state of New York, the city is the center of the New York metropolitan area, one of the most populous urban agglomerations in the world. **(Q106)** A global power city, New York City exerts a significant impact upon commerce, finance, media, art, fashion, research, technology, education, and entertainment, its fast pace defining the term New York minute. Home to the headquarters of the United Nations, New York is an important center for international diplomacy and has been described as the cultural and financial capital of the world.

Talk adapted from: https://en.wikipedia.org/wiki/New_York_City

Q104. What is the topic mainly about?
    A. New York attractions.
    B. New York history.
    C. New York population.
    D. New York importance.

Q105. According to the speaker, what is the population of New York City?
    A. 8,550,405.
    B. 8,550,504.
    C. 8,450,505.
    D. 8,554,404.

Q106. According to the talk, New York City exerts a significant impact upon …..?
    A. Commerce, finance, and media.
    B. Art, fashion, and research.
    C. Technology, education, and entertainment.
    D. All the above.

Talk 2

Q107. What type of land degradation does the speaker discuss?
  A. Radiation.
  ✗B. Desertification.
  C. Over-exploitation.
  D. None of the above.

Q108. The speaker mentioned the following terminologies EXCEPT....?
  A. Rampant.
  B. Planet's life cycle.
  C. Natural phenomenon.
  D. Global Warming.

Q109. What will the speaker probably talk about in her next lecture?
  A. Human over-exploitation.
  B. Different type of desertification.
  C. Other types of land degradation.
  D. Soil death.

TOEIC® Test: Listening & Reading

Script & Answer: Talk 2

Woman: **(Q107)** <u>Desertification</u> is a type of land degradation in which relatively dry area of land becomes increasingly arid, typically losing its bodies of water as well as vegetation and wildlife. It is caused by a variety of factors, such as through climate change and through the overexploitation of soil through humankind's undertaking. **(Q108)** <u>When deserts appear automatically over the natural course of a planet's life cycle, then it can be called a natural phenomenon; however, when deserts emerge due to the rampant and unchecked depletion of nutrients in soil that are essential for it to remain arable,</u> then a virtual "soil death" can be spoken of, which traces its cause back to human overexploitation. Alright, that's enough for today. **(Q109)** <u>Next lecture, we will talk about other types of land degradation.</u>

Talk adapted from: https://en.wikipedia.org/wiki/Desertification

Q107. What type of land degradation does the speaker discuss?
   A. Radiation.
   B. <u>Desertification.</u>
   C. Over-exploitation.
   D. None of the above.

Q108. The speaker mentioned the following terminologies EXCEPT....?
   A. Rampant.
   B. Planet's life cycle.
   C. Natural phenomenon.
   D. <u>Global Warming.</u>

Q109. What will the speaker probably talk about in her next lecture?
   A. Human over-exploitation.
   B. Different type of desertification.
   C. <u>Other types of land degradation.</u>
   D. Soil death.

Talk 3

Q110. Who is the audience for this talk?
    A. Students.
    ~~B. Employees.~~ ✓
    C. Parents.
    D. None of the above.

Q111. What does the speaker recommend in case of experiencing severe weather?
    A. Call your supervisor.
    B. Call the emergency number. ✓
    ~~C. Listen to the radio.~~
    D. Stay at home.

Q112. What should you do if you have questions regarding this policy?
    ~~A. Talk with your supervisor.~~
    B. Talk with your co-workers. ✓
    C. Wait till next day.
    D. Call a police station.

Script & Answer: Talk 3

Man: In the event that our area experiences severe weather or other emergency conditions, **(Q110)** <u>your immediate supervisor will notify you by telephone if you are not to report for work</u>. **(Q111)** <u>If you receive no call, and are still concerned, listen to radio ABCD</u>, 1170 AM for information every thirty minutes on the hour and half hour.
If the highway patrol considers conditions too hazardous for safe travel, we will close the office. However, if the office is open, we expect employees to make every effort to be at work. We consider time missed when the office is officially open as employee's personal time off. **(Q112)** <u>If you have questions regarding this policy, please speak to your immediate supervisor.</u>
Talk adapted from: http://www.writeexpress.com/announ05.html

Q110. Who is the audience for this talk?
    A. Students.
    B. <u>Employees.</u>
    C. Parents.
    D. None of the above.

Q111. What does the speaker recommend in case of experiencing severe weather?
    A. Call your supervisor.
    B. Call the emergency number.
    C. <u>Listen to the radio.</u>
    D. Stay at home.

Q112. What should you do if you have questions regarding this policy?
    A. <u>Talk with your supervisor.</u>
    B. Talk with your co-workers.
    C. Wait till next day.
    D. Call a police station.

Talk 4

Q113. What can the remaining budget be used for?
    A. Purchase office machines.
    B. Office vacation.
    C. Special items. ✓
    D. Second-hand supplies.

Q114. Which day should employees send memo's by?
    A. Monday.
    B. Wednesday. ✓
    C. Thursday.
    D. Friday.

Q115. What is the deadline for using the remaining fund?
    A. December 20.
    B. December 21. ✓
    C. December 30.
    D. December 31.

Script & Answer: Talk 4

Man: Thanks to the careful planning of department heads, **(Q113)** <u>we have a modest amount left in our capital equipment budget that can only be used for office machines</u>. **(Q114)** <u>Please indicate with a memo by Friday</u> which items you feel should have highest priority for upgrade or replacement. **(Q115)** <u>We will lose the funds if they are not used by December 31.</u>

Talk adapted from: http://www.writeexpress.com/announ22.html

Q113. What can the remaining budget be used for?
    A. <u>Purchase office machines.</u>
    B. Office vacation.
    C. Special items.
    D. Second-hand supplies.

Q114. Which day should employees send memo's by?
    A. Monday.
    B. Wednesday.
    C. Thursday.
    D. <u>Friday.</u>

Q115. What is the deadline for using the remaining fund?
    A. December 20.
    B. December 21.
    C. December 30.
    D. <u>December 31.</u>

Talk 5

Q116. Where is this automotive service located?
  A. Monterey.
  ✗B. Monroe County.   ✓
  C. Texas.
  D. England.

Q117. The company is the number one dealer in …..?
  A. Sales.
  ✗B. Service.
  C. Sales and service.
  D. None of the above.

Q118. What will happen in July?
  A. Celebration.
  ✗B. Summer refreshments.
  C. Giveaway.
  D. Discount.

Script & Answer: Talk 5

Woman: You are invited to help us celebrate 20 years of automotive service to the **(Q116)** residents of Monroe County. **(Q117)** We are happy to be the number one dealer in both sales and service for the State of Kansas. It's something we have worked hard to accomplish. Please drop in at 1600 Main Street during the month of June to enjoy summer refreshments and see the latest models. **(Q118)** While you are there, remember to register for our big July giveaway.

Talk adapted from: http://www.writeexpress.com/announ45.html

Q116. Where is this automotive service located?
    A. Monterey.
    B. Monroe County.
    C. Texas.
    D. England.

Q117. The company is the number one dealer in …..?
    A. Sales.
    B. Service.
    C. Sales and service.
    D. None of the above.

Q118. What will happen in July?
    A. Celebration.
    B. Summer refreshments.
    C. Giveaway.
    D. Discount.

Talk 6

Q119. Who is the audience for this talk?
- A. Employees.
- B. Directors.
- C. Customers.
- D. Dealers.

Q120. How long would the price change last?
- A. Short period of time.
- B. Long period of time.
- C. The speaker doesn't know.
- D. Not mentioned.

Q121. How long does it take for delivery?
- A. Few hours.
- B. One day.
- C. Two days.
- D. A week.

Script & Answer: Talk 6

Man: **(Q119)** <u>Because of a surprising rise in the cost of materials, we have tentatively raised prices on our entire stock</u>. The change is effective immediately, **(Q120)** <u>but we hope it will be temporary.</u>
You will still receive the same quality Doe merchandise, and **(Q121)** <u>we will still keep our commitment to next-day delivery</u>. Early indications suggest that when the volatile market settles, we will be able to return to an earlier pricing schedule. We appreciate your business and look forward to hearing from you again. We appreciate you as a loyal costumer as we weather the inflation storm.
Talk adapted from: http://www.writeexpress.com/sales11.html

Q119. Who is the audience for this talk?
    A. Employees.
    B. Directors.
    C. <u>Customers.</u>
    D. Dealers.

Q120. How long would the price change last?
    A. Short period of time.
    B. Long period of time.
    C. <u>The speaker doesn't know.</u>
    D. Not mentioned.

Q121. How long does it take for delivery?
    A. Few hours.
    B. <u>One day.</u>
    C. Two days.
    D. A week.

Talk 7

Q122. The new savings plan is available for?
  A. Full-time employees.
  B. Part-time employees.
  C. Directors.
  D. Customers.

Q123. To receive tax-deferred savings each month of 20%, how much should you invest from your monthly salary?
  A. 10%.
  B. 15%.
  C. 17%.
  D. 20%.

Q124. An information session will be held on?
  A. September 1.
  B. August 15.
  C. August 20.
  D. Next year.

Script & Answer: Talk 7

Man: In our ongoing efforts to improve your employee benefits, we are pleased to announce that effective September 1, **(Q122)** <u>Doe Corporation will participate in a savings plan available to all full-time employees.</u>
For anyone who saves at least 3% in the master retirement plan through payroll deduction each month, **(Q123)** <u>Doe Corporation will deposit a matching 3%. Employees may have a payroll deduction of up to 17% of their gross income each month, making a total possible tax-deferred savings each month of 20%.</u>
The benefits office will mail further information and enrollment forms to your home address. **(Q124)** <u>They will also hold a meeting on August 15</u>, to explain the program and answer questions. If you plan to participate, you must sign up before August 20.

Talk adapted from: http://www.writeexpress.com/announ23.html

Q122. The new savings plan is available for?
 A. <u>Full-time employees.</u>
 B. Part-time employees.
 C. Directors.
 D. Customers.

Q123. To receive tax-deferred savings each month of 20%, how much should you invest from your monthly salary?
 A. 10%.
 B. 15%.
 C. <u>17%.</u>
 D. 20%.

Q124. An information session will be held on?
 A. September 1.
 B. <u>August 15.</u>
 C. August 20.
 D. Next year.

Talk 8

Q125. What is the new company name?
    A. Doe Radio and Television Service.
    B. John Doe.
    C. Doe Electronic Technologies.
    D. John Doe Technologies.

Q126. Who is the founder of this company?
    A. Steve Doe.
    B. Doe John.
    C. John Doe.
    D. Tom Doe.

Q127. How much discount will be offered next month?
    A. 15%.
    B. 20%.
    C. 25%.
    D. 25.5%.

Script & Answer: Talk 8

Man: A lot has changed in the world of electronics **(Q126)** <u>since John Doe established</u> "Doe Radio and Television Service." Because we are now a leader in computers and cellular telephone service, **(Q125)** <u>we are changing our name to "Doe Electronic Technologies."</u> We think John would be pleased.
As part of this event, **(Q127)** <u>we invite you to stop by any time during the next month to receive a special 20% discount on any compact discs</u>, computer equipment, or cellular phones. It is always a pleasure to serve you.
Talk adapted from: http://www.writeexpress.com/announ15.html

Q125. What is the new company name?
     A. Doe Radio and Television Service.
     B. John Doe.
     C. <u>Doe Electronic Technologies.</u>
     D. John Doe Technologies.

Q126. Who is the founder of this company?
     A. Steve Doe.
     B. Doe John.
     C. <u>John Doe.</u>
     D. Tom Doe.

Q127. How much discount will be offered next month?
     A. 15%.
     B. <u>20%.</u>
     C. 25%.
     D. 25.5%.

Talk 9

Q128. Why did Jane win the fall sales contest?
  A. She talked with 50 clients in a month.
  B. She carefully followed the company regulations.
  C. She has a good connection with John Doe.
  D. She could have more customers.

Q129. What will Jane receive as a prize?
  A. House in Hawaii.
  B. Trip to Hawaii.
  C. Air ticket to Hawaii.
  D. Two nights in Hawaii.

Q130. When is the next contest?
  A. January.
  B. February.
  C. March.
  D. April.

Script & Answer: Talk 9

Woman: We are pleased to announce that the winner of our fall sales contest is Jane Doe. Congratulations, Jane!
(Q128) Jane was successful in securing 50 new clients in the month of November, which breaks the record held by John Doe since last January. Her achievement is particularly impressive since it happened in a month that is generally considered slow, showing once for her outstanding work **(Q129)** she will receive a trip for two to Honolulu, Hawaii. We wish her and her husband bon voyage.
again that it can be done.
(Q130) Our next contest begins in January. Get ready, the next winner may be you.
Talk adapted from: http://www.writeexpress.com/announ03.html

Q128. Why did Jane win the fall sales contest?
  A. She talked with 50 clients in a month.
  B. She carefully followed the company regulations.
  C. She has a good connection with John Doe.
  D. She could have more customers.

Q129. What will Jane receive as a prize?
  A. House in Hawaii.
  B. Trip to Hawaii.
  C. Air ticket to Hawaii.
  D. Two nights in Hawaii.

Q130. When is the next contest?
  A. January.
  B. February.
  C. March.
  D. April.

Talk 10

Q131. What will happen after August 30?
    A. Driving test.
    B. Drug test.
    C. X-ray test.
    D. Illiteracy test.

Q132. How will the test be conducted?
    A. Blood samples will be taken.
    B. Urine samples will be taken.
    C. Blood and urine samples will be taken.
    D. Either blood or urine samples will be taken.

Q133. What will happen if you test, "positive?"
    A. You will be fired from the company.
    B. You will be promoted.
    C. You will be offered treatment.
    D. You will have to test again.

Script & Answer: Talk 10

Woman: **(Q131)** Mark Incorporated will begin random drug testing after August 30. We feel strongly that our employees must be drug-free. If they are not, they need to seek treatment or different employment. **(Q132)** Either blood or urine samples will be collected to trace alcohol or drug use. All results will be strictly confidential.
(Q133) If you test positive, a representative from Human Resources will contact you. He or she will help you arrange a treatment program and rehabilitation schedule. If you are unwilling to pursue treatment or fail to meet the requirements of treatment, you will need to seek employment elsewhere. Doe Incorporated is committed to being part of a drug-free America.
Talk adapted from: http://www.writeexpress.com/announ37.html

Q131. What will happen after August 30?
    A. Driving test.
    B. Drug test.
    C. X-ray test.
    D. Illiteracy test.

Q132. How will the test be conducted?
    A. Blood samples will be taken.
    B. Urine samples will be taken.
    C. Blood and urine samples will be taken.
    D. Either blood or urine samples will be taken.

Q133. What will happen if you test, "positive?"
    A. You will be fired from the company.
    B. You will be promoted.
    C. You will be offered treatment.
    D. You will have to test again.

Talk 11

Q134. What will happen to the hiring process?
    A. It will be resumed.
    ✗B. It will be temporarily stopped.
    C. It will be permanently stopped.
    D. It will be more active.

Q135. This announcement will be most important for?
    ✗A. Current employees.
    B. Retired employees.
    C. New candidates.
    D. Clients.

Q136. What is the company currently working on?
    A. Hiring new people.
    ✗B. Evaluating its system.
    C. Launching new products.
    D. Summer break.

Script & Answer: Talk 11

Man: Please be aware that until further notice, **(Q134) (Q135)** <u>all hiring will be put on hold</u>. The current instability of the market suggests that we take time to assess our marketing strategies before we continue with expansion.
We realize that some sections were hoping to add positions by the new year, and we hope we can return to that plan soon, but caution dictates that we move more slowly for a short time. **(Q136)** <u>This would be a good time to review our procedures and find out where we might become more efficient.</u>

Talk adapted from: http://www.writeexpress.com/announ24.html

Q134. What will happen to the hiring process?
    A. It will be resumed.
    B. <u>It will be temporarily stopped.</u>
    C. It will be permanently stopped.
    D. It will be more active.

Q135. This announcement will be most important for?
    A. Current employees.
    B. Retired employees.
    C. <u>New candidates.</u>
    D. Clients.

Q136. What is the company currently working on?
    A. Hiring new people.
    B. <u>Evaluating its system.</u>
    C. Launching new products.
    D. Summer break.

Talk 12

Q137. Who is Eric Johnson?
- A. New Chief of Police.
- B. Former Chief of Police.
- C. City Governor.
- D. A lawyer.

Q138. When will his announcement be effective?
- A. In 20 years.
- B. Next year.
- C. In June.
- D. In July.

Q139. This announcement will be of more interest to?
- A. Fire department.
- B. Customer service department.
- C. Police department.
- D. Natural disasters department.

Script & Answer: Talk 12

Man: Springfield City is pleased to announce the appointment of Michael Christopher as its (Q139) new Chief of Police, (Q138) effective July 1. Michael Christopher is a 20-year veteran of our police force and was recently awarded the Governor's medal for meritorious service for his actions in thwarting a terrorist attack on City Hall. (Q137) He succeeds Eric Johnson who will retire in June after a distinguished career in law enforcement. Springfield City is fortunate to have such capable leaders in our police force.

Talk adapted from: http://www.writeexpress.com/announ20.html

Q137. Who is Eric Johnson?
- A. New Chief of Police.
- B. Former Chief of Police.
- C. City Governor.
- D. A lawyer.

Q138. When will his announcement be effective?
- A. In 20 years.
- B. Next year.
- C. In June.
- D. In July.

Q139. This announcement will be of more interest to?
- A. Fire department.
- B. Customer service department.
- C. Police department.
- D. Natural disasters department.

Talk 13

Q140. This announcement is for?
   A. Urgent meeting.
   B. Special meeting.
   C. Routine meeting.
   D. Weekly meeting.

Q141. How many reports will be covered in the meeting?
   A. One.
   B. Two.
   C. Three.
   D. Not mentioned.

Q142. What should you do if you can't attend the meeting?
   A. Submit an absence form.
   B. Call your assistant.
   C. Your assistant should replace you.
   D. Email your report.

Script & Answer: Talk 13

Man: **(Q140)** <u>We will hold our monthly research meeting</u> in the conference room at 11:00 a.m. on Friday, July 16.
John and Jane will report on the meeting with their French counterparts. Each of us should be prepared to give an update on our current projects. I think John and Jane's report will be of special interest to the additives division.
(Q142) <u>If you cannot make the meeting, be sure your assistant is prepared to give your report.</u>
Talk adapted from: http://www.writeexpress.com/announ14.html

Q140. This announcement is for?
    A. Urgent meeting.
    B. Special meeting.
    C. <u>Routine meeting.</u>
    D. Weekly meeting.

Q141. How many reports will be covered in the meeting?
    A. One.
    B. Two.
    C. Three.
    D. <u>Not mentioned.</u>

Q142. What should you do if you can't attend the meeting?
    A. Submit an absence form.
    B. Call your assistant.
    C. <u>Your assistant should replace you.</u>
    D. Email your report.

COFFEE BREAK

TOEIC READING

How to use this section of the book?

- Carefully read the question
- Choose the best answer
- Check your answer
- Look at the answer's explanation, and study TOEIC® tips
- Practice!

PART 5: INCOMPLETE SENTENCES

(30 QUESTIONS)

In this part of the test you must fill in some missing words. You will have four possible answers for each sentence; A, B, C, or D. Most sentences will be based on the form of the word – noun, verb, adverb, adjective, preposition, etc.

Examples
Q1. China Airlines flight from Tokyo …… Bangkok has been cancelled.
   (A) in
   (B) for
   (C) to
   (D) by
Answer: The correct answer is C - "to"

Q2. Everyone …….. happy.
   (A) is
   (B) are
   (C) have
   (D) were
Answer: The correct answer is A - "is." Everyone is a singular subject even though it appears to be plural. "Is" is the only available singular verb.

Strategies:

Perfect your grammar and vocabulary words! Below are some helpful grammar hints that will help you for this section.

Comparative Vs Superlative
Comparative:
Short adjective + er + than---> Ex: "A is taller than B"
More + long adjective + than---> Ex: "A is more expensive than B"
Superlative:
The + most + long adjective---> Ex: "A is the most beautiful girl in the room"
The + short adjective + est---> Ex: "A is the shortest boy in our family"

Many Vs Much
Use *many* with countable nouns (students, desks,….)
Use *much* with uncountable nouns (money, bread, water...)
Use a lot, a lot of, lots of with both countable and uncountable nouns.

Make Vs Do
Make - past tense (made) --> to create something --> Ex: I made a cake.
Do - past tense (did) --> to complete something --> Ex: I did my homework.

Adjective Vs Verb
Verb + ing = ***adjective*** --> Ex: I like the shining stars.
Verb to be (am - is - are - was - were) + verb + ing = ***verb*** -->Ex: The stars are shining.

English tenses
Present simple → He lives in Japan.
Present continuous → He is living in Japan.
Past simple → He lived in Japan.
Past continuous → He was living in Japan.
Future simple → He will live in Japan.

TOEIC ®Tenses
Depending on the preposition/time expression used, you may have to use a different past tense. The most common ones used by TOEIC® are:
Use simple past tense with ago, last, in .
Ex: We moved to Japan in 2012.
Use present perfect tense with since, lately.
Ex: We have moved to Japan since 2012.
Use past perfect tense with by .
Ex: We had moved to Japan by 2012.

Prepositions
For: Explains reason or purpose (just like "because")
And: Adds one thing to another
Nor: Used to present an alternative negative idea to an already stated
But: Shows contrast
Or: Presents an alternative or a choice
Yet: Introduces a contrasting idea that follows the preceding idea logically (similar to "but")
So: Indicates effect, result or consequence

Verb First
Usually the subject comes before the verb, however, in some cases (if the sentence starts with questions, place expressions, or negatives) the verb may come first as the following examples:
Questions: Why did you come late?
Place expression: Behind the school, is Paul's house,
Negative: Not once did she study hard.

Pronouns
Subject pronouns: I, you, he, she, it, we, you, they.
Object pronouns: Me, you, him, her, it, us, you, them.
Possessive pronouns: Mine, yours, his, hers, its, ours, theirs.

Singular Subjects
The following subjects are **SINGULAR** even though they seem plural: anybody, anyone, anything, everybody, everyone, everything, nobody, no one, nothing, somebody, someone, each + noun, every + noun.

Adjective Vs Adverb
In general, adjectives are words used to help describe the nouns, whereas adverbs are used to describe verbs
Adjective: She is beautiful.
Adverb: She sings beautifully.

Subject
Single word → School, Mary, USA
Article + noun → The student, a rabbit, some money
Adjective + noun → The black tiger, The big cat

Uncountable Nouns
Some common uncountable nouns include: water, love, money, milk, vocabulary, peace, or honey. Uncountable animals include: fish, deer, salmon, sheep, and trout. So, as an example, there is nothing called 'fishs'. You can use the word 'fish' as plural or singular, depending on the meaning of the sentence.

Prepositions
Prepositions of Place: at, on, in, by, under, near
Prepositions of Movement: to, towards, through, across
Prepositions of Time: for, at, since, after

Paired conjunctions

Paired conjunctions include: as...as; both... and; either...or; neither...nor, not only...but also.

As....as → She is <u>as</u> smart <u>as</u> her sister.
Both.... And → <u>Both</u> Jack <u>and</u> Mina are students.
Either..... or → <u>Either</u> Sally <u>or</u> Nancy will attend the party.
Neither .... Nor → <u>Neither</u> Sally <u>nor</u> Nancy will attend the party.
Not only..... but also → She is <u>not only</u> smart, <u>but also</u> beautiful.

Articles

Singular articles: A, an, another,
Plural articles: Other, some
Singular or plural articles: The, then

Notes

40 Practice Questions

Q1 – Q5

Q1. Tokyo, officially Tokyo Metropolis, …….. the capital of Japan.
  (A) are
  (B) is ✓
  (C) has
  (D) have

Q2. Star Wars, an American epic space opera franchise, ……..centered on a film series created by George Lucas.
  (A) are
  (B) is ✓
  (C) has
  (D) have

Q3. Of all the European countries, Spain ……….. the only country to have a border with an African country (Morocco).
  (A) are
  (B) is ✓
  (C) has
  (D) have

Q4. Physical science is subdivided into branches, including physics, astronomy, chemistry, and Earth science. These branches of natural science………..further divided into more specialized branches.
  (A) are
  (B) is
  (C) be ✓
  (D) more

Q5. The hottest countries in the world ……… Libya, Saudi Arabia, Iraq, Algeria, Iran, Oman, Sudan, India, Somalia, and Mexico.
  (A) are
  (B) is ✓
  (C) example of
  (D) to be

5/5

Answer: Q1 – Q5

Q1. Tokyo, officially Tokyo Metropolis, …….. the capital of Japan.
   (A) are
   (B) is
   (C) has
   (D) have
   Hint: 'Tokyo' is the subject of the sentence.

Q2. Star Wars, an American epic space opera franchise, ……..centered on a film series created by George Lucas.
   (A) are
   (B) is
   (C) has
   (D) have
   Hint: 'Star Wars' is a name of a movie, therefore, it is a singular subject.

Q3. Of all the European countries, Spain……….. the only country to have a border with an African country (Morocco).
   (A) are
   (B) is
   (C) has
   (D) have
   Hint: 'Spain' is the subject of the sentence.

Q4. Physical science is subdivided into branches, including physics, astronomy, chemistry, and Earth science. These branches of natural science………..further divided into more specialized branches.
   (A) are
   (B) is
   (C) be
   (D) more
   Hint: 'These branches' is the subject of the sentence.

Q5. The hottest countries in the world ……… Libya, Saudi Arabia, Iraq, Algeria, Iran, Oman, Sudan, India, Somalia, and Mexico.
   (A) are
   (B) is
   (C) example of
   (D) to be
   Hint: 'The hottest countries' is the subject of the sentence.

Q6 – Q10

Q6. The ………….. Loser is an American competition reality show that debuted on NBC on October 19, 2004.
- (A) most Biggest
- (B) more Bigger
- (C) Bigger than
- (D) Biggest

Q7. The Oxfam report said that the ………1% has owned more wealth than the rest of the planet since 2015.
- (A) richest
- (B) richer
- (C) most richest
- (D) more richer

Q8. "Washington is much …………… once you're here than it appears to be from the outside," said William Pierce.
- (A) complicated
- (B) most complicated
- (C) more complicated
- (D) complicated than

Q9. This is a list of … ……… people to be measured and verified, living and dead, from 1835 to the present.
- (A) tallest
- (B) taller
- (C) the tallest
- (D) the most tallest

Q10. Social science has ……….branches, each of which is considered a "social science".
- (A) much
- (B) many
- (C) both
- (D) a

Answer: Q6 – Q10

Q6. (The)………….. Loser is an American competition reality show that debuted on NBC on October 19, 2004.
 (A) most Biggest
 (B) more Bigger
 (C) Bigger than
 (D) <u>Biggest</u>

Hint: Superlative→ The + Short adjective + est

Q7. The Oxfam report said that (the)………1% has owned more wealth than the rest of the planet since 2015.
 (A) <u>richest</u>
 (B) richer
 (C) most richest
 (D) more richer

Hint: Superlative→ The + Short adjective + est

Q8. "Washington is much …………… once you're here (than) it appears to be from the outside," said William Pierce.
 (A) complicated
 (B) most complicated
 (C) <u>more complicated</u>
 (D) complicated than

Hint: Comparative→ more + long adjective + than

Q9. This is a list of ………… people to be measured and verified, living and dead, from 1835 to the present.
 (A) tallest
 (B) taller
 (C) <u>the tallest</u>
 (D) the most tallest

Hint: Superlative→ The + Short adjective + est

Q10. Social science has ……… (branches) each of which is considered a "social science".
 (A) much
 (B) <u>many</u>
 (C) both
 (D) a

Hint: Use *many* with countable nouns

Q11 – Q16

Q11. I didn't get …….. sleep that night.
  (A) much
  (B) many
  (C) both
  (D) a

Q12. The privilege to establish these four faculties was usually part of all medieval charters for universities, but not every university could ……. so in practice.
  (A) do
  (B) make
  (C) did
  (D) made

Q13. Sociolinguistics often ……. use of traditional quantitative analysis and statistics in investigating the frequency of features.
  (A) does
  (B) makes
  (C) made
  (D) did

Q14. These are very ………books.
  (A) satisfying
  (B) satisfy
  (C) satisfies
  (D) satisfied

Q15. Theresa Philips ……… the longest honeymoon period since the 1950s.
  (A) is
  (B) is enjoying
  (C) enjoying
  (D) enjoy

Q16. Last week I met my aunt; her name ….. Suzan.
  (A) is
  (B) are
  (C) was
  (D) were

Answer: Q11 – Q16

Q11. I didn't get ……. sleep that night.
(A) much
(B) many
(C) both
(D) a
Hint: Use *much* with uncountable nouns

Q12. The privilege to establish these four faculties was usually part of all medieval charters for universities, but not every university could ……. so in practice.
(A) do
(B) make
(C) did
(D) made
Hint: Do → past tense (did) --> to complete something

Q13. Sociolinguistics often …… use of traditional quantitative analysis and statistics in investigating the frequency of features.
(A) does
(B) makes
(C) made
(D) did
Hint: Make → past tense (made) --> to create something

Q14. These are very ………books.
(A) satisfying
(B) satisfy
(C) satisfies
(D) satisfied
Hint: Verb + ing = adjective

Q15. Theresa Philips ……… the longest honeymoon period since the 1950s.
(A) is
(B) is enjoying
(C) enjoying
(D) enjoy
Hint: Verb to be (am - is - are - was - were) + verb + ing = verb

Q16. Last week I met my aunt; her name ….. Suzan.
(A) is
(B) are
(C) was
(D) were
Hint: Depends on meaning, you can use both past and present tenses in the same sentence.

Q17 – Q22

Q17. They finally realized that they …… never left the Great Spirit.
(A) was
(B) are
(C) been
(D) had

Q18. They were neither cheap ….. convenient.
(A) or
(B) nor
(C) for
(D) and

Q19. It doesn't matter whether the theory is right ….. wrong.
(A) but
(B) nor
(C) or
(D) and

Q20. It was still painful …. I went to see a specialist.
(A) and
(B) so
(C) but
(D) yet

Q21. There's a phone call ….. you.
(A) on
(B) to
(C) for
(D) so

Q22. People could …….. in those days.
(A) starving
(B) starves
(C) starve
(D) starved

Answer: Q17 – Q22

Q17. They finally realized that they …… never left the Great Spirit.
   (A) was
   (B) are
   (C) been
   (D) had
          Hint: Past Perfect Tense→ Subject+ had+ past participle

Q18. They were neither cheap ….. convenient.
   (A) or
   (B) nor
   (C) for
   (D) and
          Hint: Paired conjunctions→ neither…..nor

Q19. It doesn't matter whether the theory is right ….. wrong.
   (A) but
   (B) nor
   (C) or
   (D) and
          Hint: Paired conjunctions→ whether …..or

Q20. It was still painful …. I went to see a specialist.
   (A) and
   (B) so
   (C) but
   (D) yet
          Hint: So→indicates effect, result or consequence

Q21. There's a phone call ….. you.
   (A) on
   (B) to
   (C) for
   (D) so
          Hint: For→ explains reason or purpose

Q22. People could …….. in those days.
   (A) starving
   (B) starves
   (C) starve
   (D) starved
          Hint: After modal verbs, such as "could" verb comes in the basic form.

Q23 – Q27

Q23. The song ……. out in 1980, arguably the dawn of one of the greatest musical decades every known to mankind.
   (A) come
   (B) came
   (C) has came
   (D) had came

Q24. Global temperature …….. since 1850.
   (A) change
   (B) had changed
   (C) has changed
   (D) changing

Q25. English is simpler than some languages in that it has no grammatical gender, and plurals and tenses are mostly ……...
   (A) regular
   (B) bilingual
   (C) roughly
   (D) changing

Q26. England covers five-eighths of the ……… of Great Britain (which lies in the North Atlantic) in its center and south; and includes over 100 smaller islands such as the Isles of Scilly, and the Isle of Wight.
   (A) majority
   (B) lake
   (C) island
   (D) country

Q27. The Industrial Revolution began in Great Britain and most of the important technological ………. were British.
   (A) participation
   (B) evaluation
   (C) motivation
   (D) innovations

Answer: Q23 – Q27

Q23. The song ……. out (in) 1980, arguably the dawn of one of the greatest musical decades every known to mankind.

(A) come
(B) came
(C) has came
(D) had came

Hint: Use simple past tense with 'ago, last, in'

Q24. Global temperature …….. (since) 1850.

(A) change
(B) had changed
(C) has changed
(D) changing

Hint: Use present perfect tense with 'since, lately'

Q25. English is simpler than some languages in that it has no grammatical gender, and plurals and tenses are mostly ………

(A) regular
(B) bilingual
(C) roughly
(D) changing

Hint: Regular → in order

Q26. England covers five-eighths of the ……… of Great Britain (which lies in the North Atlantic) in its center and south; and includes over 100 smaller islands such as the Isles of Scilly, and the Isle of Wight.

(A) majority
(B) lake
(C) island
(D) country

Hint: Island → landed surrounded by water

Q27. The Industrial Revolution began in Great Britain and most of the important technological ………. were British.

(A) participation
(B) evaluation
(C) motivation
(D) innovations

Hint: Innovation → something new

Q28 – Q32

Q28. A water wheel is a machine for ……… the energy of free-flowing or falling water into useful forms of power, often in a watermill.
   (A) converting
   (B) wasting
   (C) verified
   (D) submitting

Q29. Some water wheels are fed by water from a mill pond, which is formed when a flowing stream is ……….
   (A) regulated
   (B) found
   (C) dammed
   (D) dehydrated

Q30. A machine is a …….. containing one or more parts that uses energy to perform an intended action.
   (A) formalization
   (B) vender
   (C) tool
   (D) container

Q31. A vehicle is a mobile machine that transports people or cargo. Typical vehicles include wagons, bicycles, and motor ……….
   (A) civilization
   (B) endorsement
   (C) accommodation
   (D) vehicles

Q32. Ancient Egypt was a civilization of ……… Northeastern Africa, concentrated along the lower reaches of the Nile River in what is now the modern country of Egypt.
   (A) argent
   (B) ancient
   (C) industrial
   (D) vaccination

Answer: Q28 – Q32

Q28. A water wheel is a machine for ……… the energy of free-flowing or falling water into useful forms of power, often in a watermill.
 (A) <u>converting</u>
 (B) wasting
 (C) verified
 (D) submitting

Hint: Converting → changing

Q29. Some water wheels are fed by water from a mill pond, which is formed when a flowing stream is ……....
 (A) regulated
 (B) found
 (C) <u>dammed</u>
 (D) dehydrated

Hint: Dammed → stopped by a wall

Q30. A machine is a …….. containing one or more parts that uses energy to perform an intended action.
 (A) formalization
 (B) vender
 (C) <u>tool</u>
 (D) container

Hint: Tool → device

Q31. A vehicle is a mobile machine that transports people or cargo. Typical vehicles include wagons, bicycles, and motor ……...
 (A) civilization
 (B) endorsement
 (C) accommodation
 (D) <u>vehicles</u>

Hint: Vehicle → a means of carrying or transporting something

Q32. Ancient Egypt was a civilization of ……… Northeastern Africa, concentrated along the lower reaches of the Nile River in what is now the modern country of Egypt.
 (A) argent
 (B) <u>ancient</u>
 (C) industrial
 (D) vaccination

Hint: Ancient → very old

Q33 – Q37

Q33. Nomadic modern human hunter-gatherers began living in the Nile valley through the end of the Middle Pleistocene some 120,000 years ....
(A) meanwhile
(B) ago
(C) yet
(D) indeed

Q34. Shakespeare was born and brought up in Stratford-upon-Avon, Warwickshire. At the age of 18, he married Anne Hathaway, with ...... he had three children.
(A) whom
(B) who
(C) whose
(D) how

Q35. Mickey Mouse generally appears alongside his girlfriend Minnie Mouse, ... pet dog Pluto, and his friends Donald Duck and Goofy.
(A) his
(B) her
(C) their
(D) them

Q36. RMS Titanic was a British passenger liner that ...... in the North Atlantic Ocean in the early morning of 15 April 1912, after colliding with an iceberg during her maiden voyage from Southampton to New York City.
(A) survived
(B) dive
(C) sank
(D) surface

Q37. The tiger is the largest cat species, most recognizable for their pattern of dark vertical stripes on reddish-orange fur with a .... underside.
(A) undersea
(B) ramble
(C) monitor
(D) lighter

Answer: Q33 – Q37

Q33. Nomadic modern human hunter-gatherers began living in the Nile valley through the end of the Middle Pleistocene some 120,000 years …….

 (A) meanwhile
 (B) <u>ago</u>
 (C) yet
 (D) indeed

   Hint: Ago → Usually comes in the end of the sentence to express time.

Q34. Shakespeare was born and brought up in Stratford-upon-Avon, Warwickshire. At the age of 18, he married Anne Hathaway, with …… he had three children.

 (A) <u>whom</u>
 (B) who
 (C) whose
 (D) how

   Hint: Whom → should be used to refer to the object of a verb or preposition

Q35. Mickey Mouse generally appears alongside his girlfriend Minnie Mouse, ……. pet dog Pluto, and his friends Donald Duck and Goofy.

 (A) <u>his</u>
 (B) her
 (C) their
 (D) them

   Hint: His → possessive form of 'he'

Q36. RMS Titanic was a British passenger liner that …… in the North Atlantic Ocean in the early morning of 15 April 1912, after colliding with an iceberg during her maiden voyage from Southampton to New York City.

 (A) survived
 (B) dive
 (C) <u>sank</u>
 (D) surface

   Hint: Sank → past tense of 'sink' which means go under water

Q37. The tiger is the largest cat species, most recognizable for their pattern of dark vertical stripes on reddish-orange fur with a …….. underside.

 (A) undersea
 (B) ramble
 (C) monitor
 (D) <u>lighter</u>

   Hint: Lighter → not heavy/small/little

Q38 – Q40

Q38. "Composition" is the act or practice of creating a song, an instrumental music piece, a work with both singing and instruments, or another …… of music.
   (A) data
   (B) type
   (C) instrument
   (D) staff

Q39. All three curriculums …….. pitch, dynamics, timbre and texture as elements, but the other identified elements of music are far from universally agreed.
   (A) mixed
   (B) swam
   (C) identify
   (D) clash

Q40. In Western art music, the most ……. types of written notation are scores, which include all the music parts of an ensemble piece.
   (A) unknown
   (B) underesteimated
   (C) shakespearn
   (D) common

Answer: Q38 – Q40

Q38. "Composition" is the act or practice of creating a song, an instrumental music piece, a work with both singing and instruments, or another …… of music.
  (A) data
  (B) type
  (C) instrument
  (D) staff
           Hint: Type → kind

Q39. All three curriculums …….. pitch, dynamics, timbre and texture as elements, but the other identified elements of music are far from universally agreed.
  (A) mixed
  (B) swam
  (C) identify
  (D) clash
           Hint: Identify → define

Q40. In Western art music, the most ……. types of written notation are scores, which include all the music parts of an ensemble piece.
  (A) unknown
  (B) underesteimated
  (C) shakespearn
  (D) common
           Hint: Common → known

PART 6: TEXT COMPLETION

(16 QUESTIONS)

This is similar to the previous section but is on a bigger scale and has a greater focus on meaning. You need to complete three missing words or phrases but this time instead of looking at single sentences, you will complete them in a text (several sentences).

Example:

Welcome on board. We hope you will enjoy our flight to Mexico. The flight will ...... for 4 hrs.

Q1.
(A) delay
(B) last
(C) arrive
(D) fly

and you will find plenty of onboard entertainment. We will.......lunch soon.

Q2.
(A) save
(B) serve
(C) collect
(D) free

We have variety of delicious food and drink for you to choose from. Please feel free to ......

Q3.
(A) ask
(B) thank
(C) gratitude
(D) join

for assistance at any time. Once again, welcome aboard and we hope to see you again soon.

Answer:

Q1. B - "last" which means "continue for."
Q2. B - "serve" which means "give."
Q3. A - "ask" which means "request."

Strategies:
You need to double check the previous section grammar hints.

Notes

21 Practice Questions

Passage 1

Please plan to join us for a short session on how to use our new telephone system. A representative from the telephone company will be on hand in the conference room to explain the new features and to answer your questions on Friday, June 9, ….. 4:30 p.m.

Q41.
- A. at
- B. on
- C. in
- D. out

The session will be repeated at the same time Monday, June 12. We ……. all employees to attend one of these sessions.

Q42.
- A. expecting
- B. expect
- C. expected
- D. expects

Among other things we will learn how to benefit from such features as phone mail, call forwarding, conference calling, and several other new functions. …….. training will not be repeated after June 12. Please be prepared to take notes.

Q43.
- A. Then
- B. These
- C. Those
- D. This

Passage adapted from: http://www.writeexpress.com/announ46.html

Answer Passage 1

Please plan to join us for a short session on how to use our new telephone system. A representative from the telephone company will be on hand in the conference room to explain the new features and to answer your questions on Friday, June 9, ….. (4:30 p.m.)

Q41.

- A. at
- B. on
- C. in
- D. out

Hint: 'at' comes before time

The session will be repeated at the same time Monday, June 12. We ……. all employees to attend one of these sessions.

Q42.

- A. expecting
- B. expect
- C. expected
- D. expects

Hint: The subject is plural "we" and the sentence is in the present tense.

Among other things we will learn how to benefit from such features as phone mail, call forwarding, conference calling, and several other new functions. …….. (training) will not be repeated after June 12. Please be prepared to take notes.

Q43.

- A. Then
- B. These
- C. Those
- D. This

Hint: 'this' refers to singular noun or pronoun

Passage adapted from: http://www.writeexpress.com/announ46.html

Passage 2

Our warmest congratulations to Eric Johnson, who recently ……….the industry's award for the best TV commercial of the year. A recent graduate from the Mark Academy, Eric joined us in 2001 and immediately attracted the attention of writers and artists with his avant-guard style.

Q44.
    A. receive
    B. received
    C. receives
    D. receiving

He says he enjoys working in our country setting, where he and his …… can enjoy the inspiration of the mountains.

Q45.
    A. Shredder
    B. report
    C. mountain
    D. bride

The award is given each year for the commercial that industry writers and artists vote as most effective in the use …… visual media. Eric will receive his award at the annual banquet of screen and television writers in February.

Q46.
    A. in
    B. on
    C. of
    D. at

Our best wishes to Eric and to all our writers who set today's standard of excellence. Your futures look very bright.

Passage adapted from: http://www.writeexpress.com/announ32.html

Answer Passage 2

Our warmest congratulations to Eric Johnson, who recently ……….the industry's award for the best TV commercial of the year. A recent graduate from the Mark Academy, Eric joined us in 2001 and immediately attracted the attention of writers and artists with his avant-guard style.

Q44.
- A. receive
- B. <u>received</u>
- C. receives
- D. receiving

Hint: The sentence is in the past tense

He says he enjoys working in our country setting, where he and his …… can enjoy the inspiration of the mountains.

Q45.
- A. Shredder
- B. report
- C. mountain
- D. <u>bride</u>

Hint: Bride→ new wife

The award is given each year for the commercial that industry writers and artists vote as most effective in the (use) …… visual media. Eric will receive his award at the annual banquet of screen and television writers in February.

Q46.
- A. in
- B. on
- C. <u>of</u>
- D. at

Hint: Use of→ use something for a specific purpose

Our best wishes to Eric and to all our writers who set today's standard of excellence. Your futures look very bright.

Passage adapted from: http://www.writeexpress.com/announ32.html

Passage 3

It is with personal regret but ……. wishes that I announce the retirement of Jane Smith, effective May 31.

Q47.
- A. hot
- B. cold
- C. warm
- D. freezing

Jane's ……….marks the end of an era for Samuel Corporation. She was the first person to see the value of television advertising for our products, and has been on the cutting edge of marketing ever since.

Q48.
- A. leaving
- B. is leaving
- C. leaves
- D. leaved

We are indebted to her vision and commitment for propelling us to our present position in the industry. Her …….. has assured our success into the next century.

Q49.
- A. worked
- B. works
- C. working
- D. work

We will honor Jane for her contributions in a farewell reception to be held in the President's Ballroom at 7:00 to 9:00 p.m. on Friday, May 30. We invite all employees to extend their good wishes to Jane in her new endeavors.

Passage adapted from: http://www.writeexpress.com/announ35.html

Answer Passage 3

It is with personal regret but ……. wishes that I announce the retirement of Jane Smith, effective May 31.

Q47.
- A. hot
- B. cold
- C. warm
- D. freezing

Hint: Warm wishes → good luck

Jane's ………. marks the end of an era for Samuel Corporation. She was the first person to see the value of television advertising for our products, and has been on the cutting edge of marketing ever since.

Q48.
- A. leaving
- B. is leaving
- C. leaves
- D. leaved

Hint: Present continues tense → am/is/are + v+ ing

We are indebted to her vision and commitment for propelling us to our present position in the industry. Her …….. has assured our success into the next century.

Q49.
- A. worked
- B. works
- C. working
- D. work

Hint: Work → job (noun)

We will honor Jane for her contributions in a farewell reception to be held in the President's Ballroom at 7:00 to 9:00 p.m. on Friday, May 30. We invite all employees to extend their good wishes to Jane in her new endeavors.

Passage adapted from: http://www.writeexpress.com/announ35.html

Passage 4

Original Motion Picture Soundtrack now available!
We are pleased to announce to the friends and supporters of Main Street Movie Company the ………. of the Kansas soundtrack.

Q50.
    A. recreation
    B. release
    C. reunion
    D. reunited

This CD is no ordinary soundtrack. On the disk there are ……. 20 cuts of breathtaking music from the film as well as about 20 clips of dialog from the film itself. We hope you will enjoy this unique way of experiencing the film.

Q51.
    A. anticipated
    B. randomly
    C. roughly
    D. mixture

This CD will initially be available exclusively online, and will only be released in stores depending on online sales--so we ask that you …….. the word among your friends and family by forwarding this email.

Q52.
    A. spell
    B. spread
    C. count
    D. construct

Thanks to all of you. We hope you enjoy this unique soundtrack!

Passage adapted from: http://www.writeexpress.com/announ19.html

Answer Passage 4

Original Motion Picture Soundtrack now available!
We are pleased to announce to the friends and supporters of Main Street Movie Company the ………. of the Kansas soundtrack.

Q50.
- A. recreation
- B. <u>release</u>
- C. reunion
- D. reunited

Hint: Release → publish

This CD is no ordinary soundtrack. On the disk there are ……. 20 cuts of breathtaking music from the film as well as about 20 clips of dialog from the film itself. We hope you will enjoy this unique way of experiencing the film.

Q51.
- A. anticipated
- B. randomly
- C. <u>roughly</u>
- D. mixture

Hint: Roughly → about

This CD will initially be available exclusively online, and will only be released in stores depending on online sales--so we ask that you …….. the word among your friends and family by forwarding this email.

Q52.
- A. spell
- B. <u>spread</u>
- C. count
- D. construct

Hint: Spread → tell people about something

Thanks to all of you. We hope you enjoy this unique soundtrack!

Passage adapted from: http://www.writeexpress.com/announ19.html

Passage 5

Since the government has eased ……. tariffs on wool products, we have negotiated a new agreement with our Australian supplier and are pleased to pass the savings on to you.

Q53.
- A. experiment
- B. volition
- C. sell
- D. import

We …….. that the prices on most winter clothing will be reduced by about 5%.

Q54.
- A. appreciate
- B. value
- C. anticipate
- D. underestimate

You will receive a new price ……. in the near future. In the meantime, rest assured that the reduced prices are in effect for all orders postmarked after September 15.

Q55.
- A. investment
- B. catalog
- C. model
- D. map

It is a pleasure to meet your needs for quality winter wear at the lowest possible prices.

Passage adapted from: http://www.writeexpress.com/announ28.html

Answer Passage 5

Since the government has eased ……. tariffs on wool products, we have negotiated a new agreement with our Australian supplier and are pleased to pass the savings on to you.

Q53.
    A. experiment
    B. volition
    C. sell
    D. <u>import</u>

Hint: Import → buy something from another country

We …….. that the prices on most winter clothing will be reduced by about 5%.

Q54.
    A. appreciate
    B. value
    C. <u>anticipate</u>
    D. underestimate

Hint: Anticipate → expect

You will receive a new price ……. in the near future. In the meantime, rest assured that the reduced prices are in effect for all orders postmarked after September 15.

Q55.
    A. investment
    B. <u>catalog</u>
    C. model
    D. map

Hint: Catalog → list

It is a pleasure to meet your needs for quality winter wear at the lowest possible prices.

Passage adapted from: http://www.writeexpress.com/announ28.html

Passage 6

It's time to ……. my appreciation for the great friendships I have had here at Smith's over the past years. As some of you know, I am retiring at the end of May and plan to move to my old hometown of Springfield. I hope to do some writing on the history of that area before all the early residents are gone.

Q56.
- A. expressed
- B. expresses
- C. express
- D. expressing

I know John has been considering two candidates for my position, and I feel good about them both. …….. is qualified to do an excellent job. Each has a wealth of experience and both are amiable co-workers. I feel good that I am leaving my work in their capable hands.

Q57.
- A. Both
- B. Either
- C. Neither
- D. He

Leaving will not be entirely easy. I have genuinely …….. working with our great staff.

Q58.
- A. enjoyed
- B. enjoy
- C. will enjoy
- D. is enjoying

Please remember us at the summer picnic and feel welcome to drop in to see us in Springfield.

Passage adapted from: http://www.writeexpress.com/announ36.html

Answer Passage 6

It's time (to) .... my appreciation for the great friendships I have had here at Smith's over the past years. As some of you know, I am retiring at the end of May and plan to move to my old hometown of Springfield. I hope to do some writing on the history of that area before all the early residents are gone.

Q56.
- A. expressed
- B. expresses
- C. <u>express</u>
- D. expressing

Hint: After 'to' the verb comes in the basic form - nothing in the end

I know John has been considering two candidates for my position, and I feel good about them both. .... is qualified to do an excellent job. Each has a wealth of experience and both are amiable co-workers. I feel good that I am leaving my work in their capable hands.

Q57.
- A. Both
- B. <u>Either</u>
- C. Neither
- D. He

Hint: Either → two people or things share same things

Leaving will not be entirely easy. I (have) genuinely .... working with our great staff.

Q58.
- A. <u>enjoyed</u>
- B. enjoy
- C. will enjoy
- D. is enjoying

Hint: Past perfect tense → has/have + past tense

Please remember us at the summer picnic and feel welcome to drop in to see us in Springfield.

Passage adapted from: http://www.writeexpress.com/announ36.html

Passage 7

Dear Mr. Elmetaher,

Thanks for joining our affiliate program. I hope you get excited when you consider the possibilities. I can't ……. for you to get started.

Q59.
- A. wait
- B. inspire
- C. manage
- D. cooperate

And we are always open for ……… ideas. If you have any ideas that you would like to share about increasing traffic and earning larger checks, I'm here to help out. I want our affiliation to be long and profitable.

Q60.
- A. boring
- B. foolish
- C. innovative
- D. ordinary

So, let's get going! We'll make a lot of money and have fun in the process.
Best ………,
Mark Christopher

Q61.
- A. regarding
- B. regard
- C. regards
- D. regarded

Passage adapted from: http://www.writeexpress.com/welcom05.html

Answer Passage 7

Dear Mr. Elmetaher,

Thanks for joining our affiliate program. I hope you get excited when you consider the possibilities. I can't ……. for you to get started.

Q59.
- A. wait
- B. inspire
- C. manage
- D. cooperate

Hint: I can't wait → I am very happy and excited.

And we are always open for ……… ideas. If you have any ideas that you would like to share about increasing traffic and earning larger checks, I'm here to help out. I want our affiliation to be long and profitable.

Q60.
- A. boring
- B. foolish
- C. innovative
- D. ordinary

Hint: Innovative → New/creative

So, let's get going! We'll make a lot of money and have fun in the process.
Best ………,
Mark Christopher

Q61.
- A. regarding
- B. regard
- C. regards
- D. regarded

Hint: Best regards → 'best wishes' - usually used in the end of emails or letter.

Passage adapted from: http://www.writeexpress.com/welcom05.html

PART 7: READING COMPREHENSION
(54 QUESTIONS)

This is the biggest part of the reading section and contains almost half of the reading section questions. You will be asked to read an article from a magazine, letter, advertisement, or newspaper and then answer some questions.

Example
The bus schedule has changed from last month. Bus N. 5 now departs at 5:00 AM instead of 6:00 AM. Thank you to those who requested this change. Bus N. 6, 7, and 8 will take five minutes longer to complete their route as they will now pass by Victoria Square so that we can serve more people who live in the area. Finally, Bus N. 9 will run more frequently; twice per hour.

Q1. How many buses does the announcement include?
(A) 2
(B) 3
(C) 4
(D) 5
Answer: D - "5" buses, N. 5, 6, 7, 8, and 9.

Q2. What will happen to the group of buses?
(A) They will be cancelled.
(B) They will run more frequently.
(C) They will take a different route.
(D) They will start earlier.
Answer: C - "They will take a different route." The reading passage said that "Bus N. 6, 7, and 8 will take five minutes longer to complete their route as they will now pass by Victoria Square."

Q3. Which of the following would be a good time to take bus N. 9?
(A) 3:00 PM
(B) 3:15 PM
(C) 3:40 PM
(D) 3:50 PM
Answer: A -"3:00." According to the passage, bus N. 9 will run twice per hour which in this case would be 3:00 PM and 3:30 PM.

Strategies:

This part of the test is mainly based on your ability to quickly read and locate key words. I understand that there may be many words that you don't understand and of course you are not allowed to use a dictionary. However, do you really need to understand the meaning of every word? In this part of the test you should just try to read very quickly to gain a rough idea about the text. However, make sure you begin by reading the questions, not the text. Here's what you should do:

1. First, read the question.
2. Find key words in the questions (subject, verb, adjective, adverb, number, …..).
3. Find the same or similar words to that key word in the text. Then you will find the answer next to it.

Again, remember that time is very limited so you shouldn't spend more than 40 seconds on any reading question. So, what should you do if 40 seconds has passed and you still don't know the answer? Just choose the answer that you think is correct and skip to the next question. You should never leave any question blank (without an answer).

Notes

....

....

....

....

....

....

....

....

Handwritten notes:
- subscription → Abbonement
- invoice → Rechnung
- enclose → Beifügen
- schlussfolgern → infer
- widersprechen → contradict
- inference → Folgerung
- obtain → erhalten
- postpone → verlegen
- vorangehen → precede
- Gerät → appliance

> **Hint**
> The most frequent TOEIC words. Write down the meaning in your native language.

Word	Meaning	Word	Meaning
mister	Herr	invoice	Rechnung x
conference	Konferenz	brochure	
vacation	Uslaub	noon	
client	Kunde	accountant	Buchhalter x
e-book	book	clerk	Beamter x
airport	Flughafen	lobby	Interessengruppe
memo		publish	
reservation	Reservierung	résumé	
logical	logisch	enclose	beifügen x
fax	fax	applicant	
o'clock		seminar	
sincerely	aufrichtig	technician	
sometime		cloth	
website		fare	Fahrpreis x
supervisor		receipt	Quittung x
candidate		traveler	
refund	rückerstatten	caller	
goods	Waren	subway	
workshop		luggage	
downtown		shipment	
deadline		infer	schlussfolgern x
cafeteria		contradict	widersprechen x
chef		umbrella	
elevator		inference	Folgerung x
reception		cellphone	
correctly		compact	
lease		merchandise	Handel x
bicycle		receptionist	
notify	ankündigen	dentist	
preview		identification	
attendant	Teilnehmer	coupon	
subscription	Abonnement	depart	
convenient	geeignet x	reschedule	verlegen x
manual		tactic	Taktik
clue	Hinweis x	renovation	Umbau

Word	Meaning	Word	Meaning
garage		upgrade	
obtain	erhalten	precede	vorangehen
oval		replacement	
inventory	Bestand	dine	speisen
outdoor		passport	
suitcase		coworker	
destination		upcoming	
occupation	Beschäftigen	cabinet	
postpone	verschieben	appliance	Gerät
explanatory	Erklärung	keyboard	
instructor		media	
supermarket		admission	Eintritt
valid		laptop	

65 practice questions

Passage 1

On February 2, 2002, I received an invoice for $546.00 from Smith Corporation, dated January 30, 2002. Although I once had a loan from Smith, I paid the full balance on January 1, 2002. Please find enclosed a copy of my returned check endorsed by a Smith employee. According to the loan agreement, I was obligated to pay $250 per month until the loan was paid in full.

The agreement also clearly states that Smith will not charge me a penalty for prepayment of the loan. Yet the January 30 invoice indicates that the $546.00 that you are demanding is a penalty. Because of the terms of our agreement, I will not pay the amount you request. I have complied in full with our contract and I expect Smith to return my promissory note within two weeks of this letter. Thank you for your prompt attention to this oversight.

Passage adapted from: http://www.writeexpress.com/disagr01.html

Q62. What is the purpose of this letter?
   A. Pay a bill.
   B. Disagree with a bill.
   C. Show appreciation.
   D. Order a bill.

Q63. The invoice was dated ….?
   A. February 2, 2002.
   B. January 30, 2002.
   C. January 1, 2002.
   D. Not mentioned.

Q64. How much is the penalty?
   A. $546.
   B. $250.
   C. $500.
   D. None of the above.

Q65. What word is, "demanding," close in meaning to?
   A. Email.
   B. Remain.
   C. Require.
   D. complain.

Answer Passage 1

On February 2, 2002, **(Q64)** <u>I received an invoice for $546.00 from Smith Corporation,</u> **(Q63)** <u>dated January 30, 2002</u>. Although I once had a loan from Smith, I paid the full balance on January 1, 2002. Please find enclosed a copy of my returned check endorsed by a Smith employee. According to the loan agreement, I was obligated to pay $250 per month until the loan was paid in full.

The agreement also clearly states that Smith will not charge me a penalty for prepayment of the loan. Yet the January 30 invoice indicates that the $546.00 that you are **(Q65)** <u>demanding</u> is a penalty. **(Q62)** <u>Because of the terms of our agreement, I will not pay the amount you request.</u> I have complied in full with our contract and I expect Smith to return my promissory note within two weeks of this letter. Thank you for your prompt attention to this oversight.

Passage adapted from: http://www.writeexpress.com/disagr01.html

Q62. What is the purpose of this letter?
    A. Pay a bill.
    B. <u>Disagree with a bill.</u>
    C. Show appreciation.
    D. Order a bill.

Q63. The invoice was dated ….?
    A. February 2, 2002.
    B. <u>January 30, 2002.</u>
    C. January 1, 2002.
    D. Not mentioned.

Q64. How much is the penalty?
    A. <u>$546.</u>
    B. $250.
    C. $500.
    D. None of the above.

Q65. What word is, "demanding," close in meaning to?
    A. Email.
    B. Remain.
    C. <u>Require.</u>
    D. complain.

Passage 2

This month we are offering our most valued customers an exceptional opportunity to save on our most popular clothing line. Our records show that you have never ordered apparel with this label. Perhaps you were unaware that we carry the line. Well, we want to give you a chance to become acquainted with it.

We know you will enjoy our cotton/polyester blend that feels like superior quality soft wool but at a fraction of the price. For a limited time, you can purchase a faux wool sweater that is virtually impossible to tell from the real thing at a 25% reduction. Go ahead, take advantage of the opportunity. You won't be disappointed! Fill out the enclosed order form and we will rush your sweaters to you. We are pleased that you have chosen Mark's for your clothing needs.

Passage adapted from: http://www.writeexpress.com/sales04.html

Q66. For whom is this announcement important?
- A. Employees.
- B. Customers.
- C. Directors.
- D. Students.

Q67. The faux wool sweater is made of?
- A. Wool.
- B. Cotton.
- C. Polyester.
- D. Cotton/Polyester.

Q68. How much is the offered discount?
- A. Half.
- B. Third.
- C. Quarter.
- D. None.

Q69. What should you do to receive the discount?
- A. Email the sales department.
- B. Call customer service.
- C. Fill out the form.
- D. Stop by the company.

Q70. Who is Mark?
- A. The company founder.
- B. The company name.
- C. The company location.
- D. The employee name.

Answer Passage 2

(Q66) <u>This month we are offering our most valued customers an exceptional opportunity</u> to save on our most popular clothing line. Our records show that you have never ordered apparel with this label. Perhaps you were unaware that we carry the line. Well, we want to give you a chance to become acquainted with it. (Q67) <u>We know you will enjoy our cotton/polyester blend that feels like superior quality soft wool but at a fraction of the price. For a limited time, you can purchase a faux wool sweater that is virtually impossible to tell from the real thing</u> **(Q68)** <u>at a 25% reduction</u>. Go ahead, take advantage of the opportunity. You won't be disappointed! **(Q69)** <u>Fill out the enclosed order form and we will rush your sweaters to you.</u> **(Q70)** <u>We are pleased that you have chosen Mark's for your clothing needs</u>.

Passage adapted from: http://www.writeexpress.com/sales04.html

Q66. For whom is this announcement important?
  A. Employees.
  B. <u>Customers.</u>
  C. Directors.
  D. Students.

Q67. The faux wool sweater is made of?
  A. Wool.
  B. Cotton.
  C. Polyester.
  D. <u>Cotton/Polyester.</u>

Q68. How much is the offered discount?
  A. Half.
  B. Third.
  C. <u>Quarter.</u>
  D. None.

Q69. What should you do to receive the discount?
  A. Email the sales department.
  B. Call customer service.
  C. <u>Fill out the form.</u>
  D. Stop by the company.

Q70. Who is Mark?
  A. The company founder.
  B. <u>The company name.</u>
  C. The company location.
  D. The employee name.

Passage 3

My most recent order, <u>transmitted</u> by fax on November 11, contains an order for two pairs of "quilted cold-weather shop coveralls," size XL, catalog number 456-7. I found that I already have sufficient stock of these garments, so I would like to delete them from this order. Please fill the rest of the order as specified. I assume that I will simply **not be charged** for the deleted items. If the order has been processed, please credit our account **the difference, $67.89**. Thank you for your cooperation in this matter, and I apologize for any inconvenience this change may have caused.

Passage adapted from: http://www.writeexpress.com/sales04.html

Q71. What is the purpose of this letter?
  A. Make a new order.
  B. Change an order.
  C. Inquire about an order.
  D. Complain about an order.

Q72. What is the $67.89 for?
  A. Quilted cold-weather shop coveralls.
  B. Two quilted cold-weather shop coveralls.
  C. The unbilled amount.
  D. Credit card amount.

Q73. How much is the total bill?
  A. $67.89.
  B. $456.7.
  C. $ 11.
  D. Not mentioned.

Q74. What word is, "transmitted," closest in meaning to?
  A. Transfer.
  B. Sent.
  C. Emailed.
  D. Mailed.

Answer Passage 3

My most recent order, **(Q74)** <u>transmitted</u> by fax on November 11, contains an order for two pairs of "quilted cold-weather shop coveralls," size XL, catalog number 456-7. I found that I already have sufficient stock of these garments, **(Q71)** <u>so I would like to delete them from this order</u>. Please fill the rest of the order as specified. **(Q72)** <u>I assume that I will simply not be charged for the deleted items. If the order has been processed, please credit our account the difference, $67.89.</u> Thank you for your cooperation in this matter, and I apologize for any inconvenience this change may have caused.

Passage adapted from: http://www.writeexpress.com/sales04.html

Q71. What is the purpose of this letter?
   A. Make a new order.
   B. <u>Change an order.</u>
   C. Inquire about an order.
   D. Complain about an order.

Q72. What is the $67.89 for?
   A. Quilted cold-weather shop coveralls.
   B. <u>Two quilted cold-weather shop coveralls.</u>
   C. The unbilled amount.
   D. Credit card amount.

Q73. How much is the total bill?
   A. $67.89.
   B. $456.7.
   C. $ 11.
   D. <u>Not mentioned.</u>

Q74. What word is, "transmitted," closest in meaning to?
   A. Transfer.
   B. <u>Sent.</u>
   C. Emailed.
   D. Mailed.

Passage 4

During our last meeting, we came to some preliminary decisions about working together. I believe I have a good understanding of your needs and you have a clear view of my services.

Therefore, I am asking that we sign a simple Letter of Intent so we can move toward a final contract. This letter would state your intent to contract with me and to make payments according to the schedule I described in my proposal to you. Once we sign this Letter of Intent, I will begin to process the final contract.

I will call you at the end of this week to set up an <u>appointment</u> to sign the Letter of Intent. I look forward to working with you.

Passage adapted from: http://www.writeexpress.com/follow04.html

Q75. What is the purpose of this letter?
   A. Make an appointment.
   B. Offering a job.
   C. Follow-up sales appointment.
   D. Offer services.

Q76. The recipient of this letter needs to sign the, "Letter of Intent," to …?
   A. Cancel the contract.
   B. Defer the contract.
   C. Process the contract.
   D. Double the contract.

Q77. What will happen at the end of the week?
   A. Plan a meeting.
   B. Sign the contract.
   C. Receive the order.
   D. Not mentioned.

Q78. The recipient of this letter needs to?
   A. Sign a letter of intent.
   B. Sign a contract.
   C. Send an email.
   D. Call the company.

Q79. The word, "appointment," is closest in meaning to?
   A. Meeting.
   B. Concert.
   C. Conference.
   D. Interview.

Answer Passage 4

During our last meeting, we came to some preliminary decisions about working together. I believe **(Q75)** I have a good understanding of your needs and you have a clear view of my services.
Therefore, I am asking that we sign a simple Letter of Intent so we can move toward a final contract. This letter would state your intent to contract with me and to make payments according to the schedule I described in my proposal to you. **(Q76)** Once we sign this Letter of Intent, I will begin to process the final contract.
(Q77) I will call you at the end of this week to set up an **(Q79)** appointment **(Q78)** to sign the Letter of Intent. I look forward to working with you.

Passage adapted from: http://www.writeexpress.com/follow04.html

Q75. What is the purpose of this letter?
   A. Make an appointment.
   B. Offering a job.
   C. Follow-up sales appointment.
   D. Offer services.

Q76. The recipient of this letter needs to sign the, "Letter of Intent," to …?
   A. Cancel the contract.
   B. Defer the contract.
   C. Process the contract.
   D. Double the contract.

Q77. What will happen at the end of the week?
   A. Plan a meeting.
   B. Sign the contract.
   C. Receive the order.
   D. Not mentioned.

Q78. The recipient of this letter needs to?
   A. Sign a letter of intent.
   B. Sign a contract.
   C. Send an email.
   D. Call the company.

Q79. The word, "appointment," is closest in meaning to?
   A. Meeting.
   B. Concert.
   C. Conference.
   D. Interview.

Passage 5

Have you forgotten us? Sometimes it is easy to overlook our bills. We value your patronage, and hope to be able to continue our business relationship. It has come to our attention, however, that your most recent invoice is 90 days past due. You have not responded to our two previous letters. If we do not receive a minimum payment within 15 days, we will be forced to cancel your credit line with Walfield Lumber and turn the account over to collections. Your payment must be at least $450, ($400 minimum plus two $25 late fees). If you have sent a payment, kindly disregard this letter. If you cannot make a minimum payment by the prescribed date, please telephone me at 555-5555 to make other arrangements. I am confident we can come to an equitable solution.

Passage adapted from: http://www.writeexpress.com/reprim02.html

Q80. What is the purpose of this letter?
  A. Customer warning.
  B. Customer invitation.
  C. Customer payment.
  D. Customer cancelation.

Q81. When should the last payment have been made?
  A. Two months.
  B. Three months.
  C. Three and half months.
  D. Not mentioned.

Q82. How much is the expected payment?
  A. $25.
  B. $50.
  C. $400.
  D. $450.

Q83. What should the recipient of this letter do if he/she has already paid?
  A. Nothing.
  B. Make a telephone call.
  C. Email the payment receipt.
  D. Make an arrangement.

Q84. The word, "equitable," is closest in meaning to?
  A. Fair.
  B. Perfect.
  C. Unusual.
  D. Common

Answer Passage 5

Have you forgotten us? Sometimes it is easy to overlook our bills. We value your patronage, and hope to be able to continue our business relationship. **(Q81)** <u>It has come to our attention, however, that your most recent invoice is 90 days past due.</u> You have not responded to our two previous letters. **(Q80)** <u>If we do not receive a minimum payment within 15 days, we will be forced to cancel your credit line with Walfield Lumber and turn the account over to collections.</u> **(Q82)** <u>Your payment must be at least $450, ($400 minimum plus two $25 late fees).</u> **(Q83)** <u>If you have sent a payment, kindly disregard this letter.</u> If you cannot make a minimum payment by the prescribed date, please telephone me at 555-5555 to make other arrangements. I am confident we can come to an **(Q84)** <u>equitable</u> solution.

Passage adapted from: http://www.writeexpress.com/reprim02.html

Q80. What is the purpose of this letter?
   A. <u>Customer warning.</u>
   B. Customer invitation.
   C. Customer payment.
   D. Customer cancelation.

Q81. When should the last payment have been made?
   A. Two months.
   B. <u>Three months.</u>
   C. Three and half months.
   D. Not mentioned.

Q82. How much is the expected payment?
   A. $25.
   B. $50.
   C. $400.
   D. <u>$450.</u>

Q83. What should the recipient of this letter do if he/she has already paid?
   A. <u>Nothing.</u>
   B. Make a telephone call.
   C. Email the payment receipt.
   D. Make an arrangement.

Q84. The word, "equitable," is closest in meaning to?
   A. <u>Fair.</u>
   B. Perfect.
   C. Unusual.
   D. Common

Passage 6

Are you tired of winter? Are you dying to get away for a dream vacation? Doe Travel is pleased to offer six exciting vacation packages at unheard of low prices. Enclosed with this letter are six brochures describing each vacation package. Call now at 555-5555 to reserve your spot. But hurry--this can't last!

Passage adapted from: http://www.writeexpress.com/sales15.html

Package	Destination	Cost per person
Hollywood	USA	$2,000
Pyramids	Egypt	$1,000
Eiffel Tower	France	$1,500
African Safari	South Africa	$2,500
Taj Mahal	India	$1,000
Big Ben	England	$3,000
25% discount if your purchase a vacation package for four or more people		

Q85. According to the ad, what is the common feature of all the offered vacation packages?
 A. Family attractions.
 B. Cheap price.
 C. Undiscovered places.
 D. Good for summer vacation.

Q86. How much would the most expensive trip be for four persons?
 A. $3000.
 B. $12,000.
 C. $9,000.
 D. $15,000.

Q87. What should you do if you want to take an advantage of this opportunity?
 A. Call the embassy.
 B. Contact the travel agency.
 C. Apply for a visa.
 D. Pay the initial cost.

Q88. How much would it cost for a family of four to spend a vacation in Egypt?
 A. $1000.
 B. $2000.
 C. $3000.
 D. $4000.

Q89. The word, "spot," is closest in meaning to?
 A. Country.
 B. Package.
 C. Flight.
 D. Price.

Answer Passage 6

Are you tired of winter? Are you dying to get away for a dream vacation? **(Q85)** Doe Travel is pleased to offer six exciting vacation packages at unheard of low prices. Enclosed with this letter are six brochures describing each vacation package. **(Q87)** Call now at 555-5555 to reserve your **(Q89)** spot. But hurry--this can't last!

Passage adapted from: http://www.writeexpress.com/sales15.html

Package	Destination	Cost per person
Hollywood	USA	$2000
(Q88*) Pyramids	Egypt	$1000
Eiffel Tower	France	$1500
African Safari	South Africa	$2500
Taj Mahal	India	$1000
(Q86+) Big Ben	England	$3000
(Q86+) (Q88*) 25% discount if your purchase a vacation package for four or more people		

Q85. According to the ad, what is the common feature of all the offered vacation packages?
 A. Family attractions.
 B. Cheap price.
 C. Undiscovered places.
 D. Good for summer vacation.

Q86. How much would the most expensive trip be for four persons?
 A. $3000.
 B. $12,000.
 C. $9,000.
 D. $15,000.

Q87. What should you do if you want to take an advantage of this opportunity?
 A. Call the embassy.
 B. Contact the travel agency.
 C. Apply for a visa.
 D. Pay the initial cost.

Q88. How much would it cost for a family of four to spend a vacation in Egypt?
 A. $1000.
 B. $2000.
 C. $3000.
 D. $4000.

Q89. The word, "spot," is closest in meaning to?
 A. Country.
 B. Package.
 C. Flight.
 D. Price.

Passage 7

I am pleased to accept your offer to join MIW Corporation as a "marketing representative." The meeting with your marketing staff convinced me that I will be working with a successful team in a dynamic company, and I look forward to contributing to the team's efforts. As you requested, I have signed and enclosed the contract which details my salary as well as commission bonuses.

I appreciate the literature you sent on the company's retirement and insurance programs. Thanks also for offering to answer questions I may have concerning these benefits, when I report to you for orientation at 8:00 a.m. on Monday, January 3. I appreciate your help in processing the employment papers and look forward to our January meeting.

Passage adapted from: http://www.writeexpress.com/accept01.html

Q90. Which team may the sender join?
   A. Corporation.
   B. Representatives.
   C. Marketing.
   D. Dynamic.

Q91. What is included with the letter?
   A. Contract.
   B. Salary.
   C. Commission.
   D. Bonuses.

Q92. In case of having questions, what should the applicant do?
   A. Make a telephone inquiry.
   B. Send an email.
   C. Wait till the orientation day.
   D. Contact his immediate supervisor.

Q93. The word, "report," is closest in meaning to?
   A. Submit.
   B. Meet.
   C. Certificate.
   D. Start.

Answer Passage 7

I am pleased to accept your offer to join MIW Corporation as a "marketing representative." **(Q90)** The meeting with your marketing staff convinced me that I will be working with a successful team in a dynamic company, and I look forward to contributing to the team's efforts. As you requested, **(Q91)** I have signed and enclosed the contract which details my salary as well as commission bonuses.
I appreciate the literature you sent on the company's retirement and insurance programs. **(Q92)** Thanks also for offering to answer questions I may have concerning these benefits, when I **(Q93)** report to you for orientation at 8:00 a.m. on Monday, January 3. I appreciate your help in processing the employment papers and look forward to our January meeting.
Passage adapted from: http://www.writeexpress.com/accept01.html

Q90. Which team may the sender join?
    A. Corporation.
    B. Representatives.
    C. Marketing.
    D. Dynamic.

Q91. What is included with the letter?
    A. Contract.
    B. Salary.
    C. Commission.
    D. Bonuses.

Q92. In case of having questions, what should the applicant do?
    A. Make a telephone inquiry.
    B. Send an email.
    C. Wait till the orientation day.
    D. Contact his immediate supervisor.

Q93. The word, "report," is closest in meaning to?
    A. Submit.
    B. Meet.
    C. Certificate.
    D. Start.

Passage 8

The events of this past week might have left some ambiguity concerning our priorities. To move forward as a team, we must remove any uncertainties and accept the challenges that lie ahead. Let me restate our decisions. First, we must meet the October 15 deadline. Our holiday sales depend on that date. Second, we must release a quality product. We realize this might require long hours and time away from your families. We want to make it up to your families and are formulating a completion bonus.

We have the best team in the industry. We are close to the finish line and can see the flags waving ahead. We need one last burst of energy and commitment from each of you. For now, stop working, go home, and take the remainder of the day off. Tomorrow we'll meet in the main conference room at 8:00 a.m. for a kick-off meeting to begin the last stretch of the race.

Passage adapted from: http://www.writeexpress.com/confir21.html

Q94. What is the purpose of this letter?
- A. Create priorities.
- B. Call for a meeting.
- C. Make an appointment.
- D. Confirm a decision.

Q95. How many goals have been set up to achieve?
- A. One.
- B. Two.
- C. Three.
- D. Four.

Q96. What kind of award would the recipients of this letter receive?
- A. Long hours.
- B. Vacation with family.
- C. Extra payment.
- D. Not mentioned.

Q97. What should the recipients of this letter do for now?
- A. Work harder.
- B. Relax at home.
- C. Attend a meeting.
- D. Make a conference.

Q98. Why has a new meeting been scheduled?
- A. To do some kicking.
- B. To start a project.
- C. To report the project results.
- D. To stretch before the race.

Answer Passage 8

The events of this past week might have left some ambiguity concerning our priorities. To move forward as a team, we must remove any uncertainties and accept the challenges that lie ahead. **(Q94)** Let me restate our decisions. **(Q95)** First, we must meet the October 15 deadline. Our holiday sales depend on that date. Second, we must release a quality product. We realize this might require long hours and time away from your families. **(Q96)** We want to make it up to your families and are formulating a completion bonus.

We have the best team in the industry. We are close to the finish line and can see the flags waving ahead. We need one last burst of energy and commitment from each of you. **(Q97)** For now, stop working, go home, and take the remainder of the day off. **(Q98)** Tomorrow we'll meet in the main conference room at 8:00 a.m. for a kick-off meeting to begin the last stretch of the race.

Passage adapted from: http://www.writeexpress.com/confir21.html

Q94. What is the purpose of this letter?
- A. Create priorities.
- B. Call for a meeting.
- C. Make an appointment.
- D. Confirm a decision.

Q95. How many goals have been set up to achieve?
- A. One.
- B. Two.
- C. Three.
- D. Four.

Q96. What kind of award would the recipients of this letter receive?
- A. Long hours.
- B. Vacation with family.
- C. Extra payment.
- D. Not mentioned.

Q97. What should the recipients of this letter do for now?
- A. Work harder.
- B. Relax at home.
- C. Attend a meeting.
- D. Make a conference.

Q98. Why has a new meeting been scheduled?
- A. To do some kicking.
- B. To start a project.
- C. To report the project results.
- D. To stretch before the race.

Passage 9
Jane Johnson, died May 6, 2001 at the Regional Medical Center in Springfield, Kansas, after a long illness. She was born January 11, 1931, in Springfield, the daughter of Marvin Blaine and Violet Smith Johnson. She was a member of the local Methodist Church and an officer in the Daughters of the American Revolution. She served for 30 years as a real estate agent in the Springfield area.

She is survived by three sons and one daughter: John, Eric, and Blaine, all of Springfield, and Michelle (Mimsy) Peck of Appledale; 11 grandchildren; two sisters and one brother: Ruth Adams, Denver, Colorado; Joyce Anderson, Colton, Kansas; Harry Johnson, Martinsville, Indiana. She was preceded in death by her husband, John Doe, and her daughter, Jane.

Funeral services will be held Thursday at 11 a.m. at the Springfield Funeral Home, 2300 Riverdale Avenue. Friends may call at the funeral home Wednesday evening from 6 to 8 p.m. or one hour prior to the services. Interment will be in the Springfield City Cemetery.

Passage adapted from: http://www.writeexpress.com/announ43.html

Q99. How old was Jane Johnson when she passed away?
  A. 30 years.
  B. 60 years.
  C. 65 years.
  D. 70 years.

Q100. How many children did Jane Johnson have?
  A. One.
  B. Two.
  C. Three.
  D. Four.

Q101. In total, how many hours are dedicated for friends' calls?
  A. One.
  B. Two.
  C. Three.
  D. Four.

Q102. The word, "Cemetery," is closest in meaning to?
  A. Ceremony.
  B. Hall.
  C. Funeral.
  D. A burial ground.

Answer Passage 9

(Q99) <u>Jane Johnson, died May 6, 2001 at the Regional Medical Center in Springfield, Kansas, after a long illness. She was born January 11, 1931</u>, in Springfield, the daughter of Marvin Blaine and Violet Smith Johnson. She was a member of the local Methodist Church and an officer in the Daughters of the American Revolution. She served for 30 years as a real estate agent in the Springfield area.

(Q100) <u>She is survived by three sons and one daughter</u>: John, Eric, and Blaine, all of Springfield, and Michelle (Mimsy) Peck of Appledale; 11 grandchildren; two sisters and one brother: Ruth Adams, Denver, Colorado; Joyce Anderson, Colton, Kansas; Harry Johnson, Martinsville, Indiana. She was preceded in death by her husband, John Doe, and her daughter, Jane.

Funeral services will be held Thursday at 11 a.m. at the Springfield Funeral Home, 2300 Riverdale Avenue. **(Q101)** <u>Friends may call at the funeral home Wednesday evening from 6 to 8 p.m. or one hour prior to the services.</u> Interment will be in the Springfield City **(Q102)** <u>Cemetery</u>.

Passage adapted from: http://www.writeexpress.com/announ43.html

Q99. How old was Jane Johnson when she passed away?
- A. 30 years.
- B. 60 years.
- C. 65 years.
- D. <u>70 years.</u>

Q100. How many children did Jane Johnson have?
- A. One.
- B. Two.
- C. Three.
- D. <u>Four.</u>

Q101. In total, how many hours are dedicated for friends' calls?
- A. One.
- B. Two.
- C. <u>Three.</u>
- D. Four.

Q102. The word, "Cemetery," is closest in meaning to?
- A. Ceremony.
- B. Hall.
- C. Funeral.
- D. <u>A burial ground.</u>

Passage 10

August 10th, 2017

I am sorry to inform you that I have decided to resign from my position as a computer programmer in order to seek a more rewarding position elsewhere. This resignation must become effective no later than two weeks from today's date.

I have concluded that my contributions here are unrewarded and my ideas ignored. I have much to offer and feel frustrated that I am consistently passed over for special projects. It is important to me to work for a company that encourages creativity rather than restricts it. Although your compensation has been fair, you have been unable to provide other types of incentives that I need.

Nevertheless, my time here has not been wasted. I have gained experience and have honed my skills. I have worked with a dedicated group who has earned my respect and admiration. I sincerely wish co-workers well in their future endeavors.

Because you have indicated that my work is excellent, I would appreciate a positive recommendation from you should any prospective employers inquire about my qualifications. If you feel you are unable to satisfy this request, I would sincerely value an opportunity to discuss with you any reservations you may have.

Yours, William Christopher

Passage adapted from: http://www.writeexpress.com/resign07.html

Q103. What is this letter for?
- A. Hiring.
- B. Resignation.
- C. Awarding.
- D. Invitation.

Q104. What is the last day for this letter to be effective?
- A. August 10th.
- B. August 15th.
- C. August 25th.
- D. Not mentioned.

Q105. What does the sender think about his position?
- A. Rewarded.
- B. Unique.
- C. Unpleasant.
- D. Excited.

Q106. What does the sender ask for?
- A. Higher salary.
- B. Good reference.
- C. Different job.
- D. Better qualifications.

Answer Passage 10

(Q104*) August 10th, 2017

I am sorry to inform you that **(Q103)** <u>I have decided to resign from my position</u> as a computer programmer in order to seek a more rewarding position elsewhere. **(Q104*)** <u>This resignation must become effective no later than two weeks from today's date.</u> **(Q105)** <u>I have concluded that my contributions here are unrewarded and my ideas ignored. I have much to offer and feel frustrated that I am consistently passed over for special projects.</u> It is important to me to work for a company that encourages creativity rather than restricts it. Although your compensation has been fair, you have been unable to provide other types of incentives that I need. Nevertheless, my time here has not been wasted. I have gained experience and have honed my skills. I have worked with a dedicated group who has earned my respect and admiration. I sincerely wish co-workers well in their future endeavors. Because you have indicated that my work is excellent, **(Q106)** <u>I would appreciate a positive recommendation from you should any prospective employers inquire about my qualifications.</u> If you feel you are unable to satisfy this request, I would sincerely value an opportunity to discuss with you any reservations you may have.

Yours, William Christopher

Passage adapted from: http://www.writeexpress.com/resign07.html

Q103. What is this letter for?
   A. Hiring.
   B. <u>Resignation.</u>
   C. Awarding.
   D. Invitation.

Q104. What is the last day for this letter to be effective?
   A. August 10th.
   B. August 15th.
   C. <u>August 25th.</u>
   D. Not mentioned.

Q105. What does the sender think about his position?
   A. Rewarded.
   B. Unique.
   C. <u>Unpleasant.</u>
   D. Excited.

Q106. What does the sender ask for?
   A. Higher salary.
   B. <u>Good reference.</u>
   C. Different job.
   D. Better qualifications.

Passage 11

Dear Ms. Christopher,

I am writing to request a copy of my graduation certificate awarded in the spring commencement services. Unfortunately, I lost the original when my briefcase was stolen from my car. I am enclosing a copy of the police report to support my claim, along with a certified check for $27.50 to cover the replacement fee. My name and other identifying information are included in the report. Please send the certificate to the address: Japan, Tokyo, apartment 405.

Thank you for your assistance.

Passage adapted from: http://www.writeexpress.com/reques11.html

Q107. What is the purpose of this letter?
  A. Reporting a stolen briefcase.
  B. Requesting a certificate replacement.
  C. Sending a tuition check.
  D. Asking for commencement services.

Q108. What does the sender enclose with the letter?
  A. Police report.
  B. Check.
  C. Police report and check.
  D. Nothing.

Q109. What is the $27.50 for?
  A. Certification fees.
  B. Issuing fees.
  C. Commencement fees.
  D. Participation fees.

Q110. What is the sender's name?
  A. Christopher.
  B. Mentioned in the check.
  C. Mentioned in the report.
  D. Not mentioned.

Q111. The new certificate should be?
  A. Emailed.
  B. Faxed.
  C. Wired.
  D. Mailed.

Passage 11

Dear Ms. Christopher,

(Q107) I am writing to request a copy of my graduation certificate awarded in the spring commencement services. Unfortunately, I lost the original when my briefcase was stolen from my car. **(Q108)** I am enclosing a copy of the police report to support my claim, along with a certified check for **(Q109)** $27.50 to cover the replacement fee. **(Q110)** My name and other identifying information are included in the report. **(Q111)** Please send the certificate to the address: Japan, Tokyo, apartment 405. Thank you for your assistance.

Passage adapted from: http://www.writeexpress.com/reques11.html

Q107. What is the purpose of this letter?
- A. Reporting a stolen briefcase.
- B. Requesting a certificate replacement.
- C. Sending a tuition check.
- D. Asking for commencement services.

Q108. What does the sender enclose with the letter?
- A. Police report.
- B. Check.
- C. Police report and check.
- D. Nothing.

Q109. What is the $27.50 for?
- A. Certification fees.
- B. Issuing fees.
- C. Commencement fees.
- D. Participation fees.

Q110. What is the sender's name?
- A. Christopher.
- B. Mentioned in the check.
- C. Mentioned in the report.
- D. Not mentioned.

Q111. The new certificate should be?
- A. Emailed.
- B. Faxed.
- C. Wired.
- D. Mailed.

Passage 12

Dear Marry,

Due to a conflict with a family commitment that night, I regret that I will be unable to attend the Mark Corporation's annual Christmas party. I didn't realize when I accepted the invitation that Johnny's school play was the same night, and we would both be very disappointed if I didn't attend. He has been practicing his part for weeks.

I am truly sorry to have to miss the party because it is one of the highlights of the holiday season. I hope I will have another chance to attend next year. Thank you so much for your kind invitation, and please accept my sincere apology for being unable to attend.

Sincerely,
Michael

Passage adapted from: http://www.writeexpress.com/cancel04.html

Q112. Why did Michael send this letter?
  A. Request an invitation.
  B. Invite family members.
  C. Cancel an invitation.
  D. Send an invitation.

Q113. What would Michael probably attend?
  A. Christmas party.
  B. Family party.
  C. Mark Corporation.
  D. School play.

Q114. When would Michael probably attend the Christmas party?
  A. Last year.
  B. This year.
  C. Next year.
  D. In two years.

Q115. The word, "commitment," is closest in meaning to??
  A. Engagement.
  B. Community.
  C. Visiting.
  D. Relatives.

Answer Passage 12

Dear Marry,

Due to a conflict with a family **(Q115)** commitment that night, **(Q112)** I regret that I will be unable to attend the Mark Corporation's annual Christmas party. I didn't realize when I accepted the invitation that **(Q113)** Johnny's school play was the same night, and we would both be very disappointed if I didn't attend. He has been practicing his part for weeks.

I am truly sorry to have to miss the party because it is one of the highlights of the holiday season. **(Q114)** I hope I will have another chance to attend next year. Thank you so much for your kind invitation, and please accept my sincere apology for being unable to attend.

Sincerely,
Michael

Passage adapted from: http://www.writeexpress.com/cancel04.html

Q112. Why did Michael send this letter?
 A. Request an invitation.
 B. Invite family members.
 C. Cancel an invitation.
 D. Send an invitation.

Q113. What would Michael probably attend?
 A. Christmas party.
 B. Family party.
 C. Mark Corporation.
 D. School play.

Q114. When would Michael probably attend the Christmas party?
 A. Last year.
 B. This year.
 C. Next year.
 D. In two years.

Q115. The word, "commitment," is closest in meaning to??
 A. Engagement.
 B. Community.
 C. Visiting.
 D. Relatives.

Passage 13

John Doe
1600 Main Street
Springfield

We have just received our county tax notice (reference #12345) indicating that our home is now valued at $161,000. This is surely an error. Just three months ago we had it appraised for a second mortgage and its market value was determined to be $130,000. I am enclosing a copy of that appraisal, along with evidence that similar homes in our neighborhood have recently sold for about $130,000.

I request that you correct our notice to reflect the actual value on which we are to be taxed. If this correspondence is not sufficient to justify the correction, please let me know what I need to do. I trust this change can be made before my taxes are due. My tax identification number is 555-55-5555.

Passage adapted from: http://www.writeexpress.com/errors10.html

Q116. What is the purpose of this letter?
A. Pay tax.
B. Selling an apartment.
C. Request a new tax form.
D. Correct an official mistake.

Q117. Based on the tax notice, how much is the house value?
A. $161,000.
B. $130,000.
C. $191,000.
D. $31,000.

Q118. What does John hope for?
A. To receive the tax return.
B. To sell his house as soon as possible.
C. To have the correction before the tax due.
D. To receive his tax identification number.

Q119. The word, "sufficient," is closest in meaning to?
A. Important.
B. Official.
C. Suffer.
D. Enough.

Passage 13

John Doe
1600 Main Street
Springfield

(Q117) We have just received our county tax notice (reference #12345) indicating that our home is now valued at $161,000. **(Q116)** This is surely an error. Just three months ago we had it appraised for a second mortgage and its market value was determined to be $130,000. I am enclosing a copy of that appraisal, along with evidence that similar homes in our neighborhood have recently sold for about $130,000.

I request that you correct our notice to reflect the actual value on which we are to be taxed. If this correspondence is not **(Q119)** sufficient to justify the correction, please let me know what I need to do. **(Q118)** I trust this change can be made before my taxes are due.
My tax identification number is 555-55-5555.

Passage adapted from: http://www.writeexpress.com/errors10.html

Q116. What is the purpose of this letter?
   A. Pay tax.
   B. Selling an apartment.
   C. Request a new tax form.
   D. Correct an official mistake.

Q117. Based on the tax notice, how much is the house value?
   A. $161,000.
   B. $130,000.
   C. $191,000.
   D. $31,000.

Q118. What does John hope for?
   A. To receive the tax return.
   B. To sell his house as soon as possible.
   C. To have the correction before the tax due.
   D. To receive his tax identification number.

Q119. The word, "sufficient," is closest in meaning to?
   A. Important.
   B. Official.
   C. Suffer.
   D. Enough.

Passage 14

To: Mr. Kent
From: Mary Smith
My husband, John Smith, and I authorize you to act on our behalf in defending us in the tax matter that we discussed with you last week.
The information on the enclosed diskette includes all of our income records for the past four years. Also enclosed are receipts, bank statements, other financial records, and a brief summary sheet.
We agree to your fee of $200 per hour. Please inform us immediately if you are willing to represent us.
Mary Smith

Passage adapted from: http://www.writeexpress.com/author02.html

Q120. What does Ms. Smith request?
  A. Marriage certificate.
  B. Tax return.
  C. Tax representative.
  D. Legal advice.

Q121. What does the diskette include?
  A. Reports.
  B. Official authorization.
  C. Financial documents.
  D. Fees.

Q122. How much might Mary be charged?
  A. It is free of charge.
  B. A hundred dollar per hour.
  C. Couple of hundred dollars per hour.
  D. Not mentioned.

Q123. What is Mary expecting?
  A. Mr. Kent's confirmation.
  B. Mr. Kent's withdrawal.
  C. Mr. Kent's bill.
  D. Mr. Kent's appreciation.

Answer Passage 14

To: Mr. Kent
From: Mary Smith
My husband, John Smith, and **(Q120)** I authorize you to act on our behalf in defending us in the tax matter that we discussed with you last week.
(Q121) The information on the enclosed diskette includes all of our income records for the past four years. Also enclosed are receipts, bank statements, other financial records, and a brief summary sheet.
(Q122) We agree to your fee of $200 per hour. **(Q123)** Please inform us immediately if you are willing to represent us.
Mary Smith

Passage adapted from: http://www.writeexpress.com/author02.html

Q120. What does Ms. Smith request?
  A. Marriage certificate.
  B. Tax return.
  C. Tax representative.
  D. Legal advice.

Q121. What does the diskette include?
  A. Reports.
  B. Official authorization.
  C. Financial documents.
  D. Fees.

Q122. How much might Mary be charged?
  A. It is free of charge.
  B. A hundred dollar per hour.
  C. Couple of hundred dollars per hour.
  D. Not mentioned.

Q123. What is Mary expecting?
  A. Mr. Kent's confirmation.
  B. Mr. Kent's withdrawal.
  C. Mr. Kent's bill.
  D. Mr. Kent's appreciation.

Passage 15

What would you pay for peace of mind? As your family's main financial support, you are naturally concerned about their future should anything happen to you. SMS Insurance offers the coverage you need to provide your family with security in the event that you are unable to.

In 10 years, you will receive a ten thousand times of each monthly dollar you pay. Our enclosed chart outlines a sampling of the benefits available through our family plans. Please fill out the enclosed information card, and one of our agents will be happy to explain what you may be missing. Of course, there is no obligation, but knowledge can bring peace of mind. We would be happy to help you.

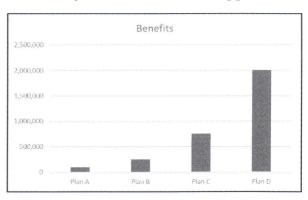

Passage adapted from: http://www.writeexpress.com/sales24.html

Q124. For plan D, how much is the monthly payment?
  A. $50.
  B. $100.
  C. $200.
  D. $250.

Q125. What are the obligations for those family plans?
  A. Knowledge.
  B. Agents.
  C. Age.
  D. None.

Q126. Which plan(s) would fit a family with a benefits goal of under half a million dollars?
  A. Plan A.
  B. Plan B.
  C. Plans A and B.
  D. Plans C and D.

Q127. What should you do to enroll in a family plan?
  A. Fill out a form.
  B. Email an inquiry card.
  C. Ask for support.
  D. Call an agent.

Answer Passage 15

What would you pay for peace of mind? As your family's main financial support, you are naturally concerned about their future should anything happen to you. SMS Insurance offers the coverage you need to provide your family with security in the event that you are unable to.

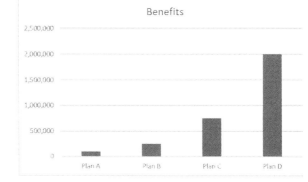

(Q124) In 10 years, you will receive a ten thousand times of each monthly dollar you pay. Our enclosed chart outlines a sampling of the benefits available through our family plans.

(Q127) Please fill out the enclosed information card, and one of our agents will be happy to explain what you may be missing.

(Q125) Of course, there is no obligation, but knowledge can bring peace of mind. We would be happy to help you.

Passage adapted from: http://www.writeexpress.com/sales24.html

Q124. For plan D, how much is the monthly payment?
- A. $50.
- B. $100.
- C. $200.
- D. $250.

Q125. What are the obligations for those family plans?
- A. Knowledge.
- B. Agents.
- C. Age.
- D. None.

Q126. Which plan(s) would fit a family with a benefits goal of under half a million dollars?
- A. Plan A.
- B. Plan B.
- C. Plans A and B.
- D. Plans C and D.

Q127. What should you do to enroll in a family plan?
- A. Fill out a form.
- B. Email an inquiry card.
- C. Ask for support.
- D. Call an agent.

APPENDIX
Frequently Asked Questions

Q1. What is the difference between TOEIC, TOEFL, and IELTS?

Both TOEFL and IELTS are international English tests for academic purposes; usually for graduate studies, internships, or exchange programs. TOEFL is American, whereas IELTS is British. On the other hand, TOEIC is mainly used for employment purposes. It is usually taken by those who would like to work for international companies where English is the primary working language. In other words, TOEIC is a way to demonstrate your English proficiency to future employers.

Q2. How many TOEIC tests are available?

TOEIC was initially started as a reading and listening test and has recently been further developed. The listening and reading test is scored as 5 to 495 points for listening and another 5 to 495 for reading with a maximum score of 990. There is also a speaking and writing version of the TOEIC test although it is not as popular. Each test has its own grading and scoring system.

Q3. Where can I take the TOEIC test? How long is it valid for?

Please check the ETS website on https://www.ets.org/toeic for test locations and fees. The test score is valid for two years.

Q4. What is the TOEIC Bridge?

TOEIC Bridge is a mini TEOIC test. It has half of the questions and can be completed in just one hour. However, it is not an official test and the scores are not valid. It is used by some universities and education institutions as a placement or progress test.

Q5. Where can I find the audio that goes along with this textbook?

The audio is provided on the following link: https://goo.gl/k4mdMJ

TEST DAY TIPS

On the night before the test day you should...
- Quickly review this textbook
- Set 2 alarms
- Go to bed early

On the test day....
- Wake up early
- Bring 2 or 3 pencils and a sharpener
- Bring an eraser
- Bring your student ID, if any
- Wear a watch
- Arrive at the testing institution early
- Don't read any study materials before the test
- Stay awake during the test

After the test...
- Have confidence in your performance
- Don't review the questions

CONTACT US

If you have any questions, comments, or suggestions, you may contact us through the following e-mail address: EnjoyTOEIC@gmail.com

спасибо 谢谢
GRACIAS
THANK YOU
ありがとうございました MERCI
DANKE धन्यवाद
شُكرًا OBRIGADO

Printed in Poland
by Amazon Fulfillment
Poland Sp. z o.o., Wrocław